MY KITCHEN
CHALKBOARD

Seasonal Menus for
MODERN NEW ENGLAND FAMILIES

MY KITCHEN
CHALKBOARD

Seasonal Menus for
MODERN NEW ENGLAND FAMILIES

Leigh Belanger

UNION PARK
PRESS

BOSTON

ALSO BY LEIGH BELANGER

The Boston Homegrown Cookbook:
Local Food, Local Restaurants, Local Recipes

Union Park Press
P.O. Box 81435
Wellesley, MA 02481

Printed in the U.S.A.
First Edition

Library of Congress Cataloging-in-Publication Data available
upon request.

Photographs by Tara Morris **www.taramorrisimages.com**
Book and cover design by Vale Hill Creative **www.valehillcreative.com**

UNION PARK | **unionparkpress.com**
PRESS | KEEPING BOOKS IN STYLE SINCE 2007

For my father, John, in whose memory I will never miss an opportunity to eat more than my share of shellfish.

WITH THANKS:

I'm filled with gratitude just thinking about the people who made this book possible. Nicole Vecchiotti and Shelby Larsson and their team at Union Park Press had the vision to turn my kitchen chalkboard into a book, and were first-rate collaborators along the way. Speaking of killer collaborators, thank you to the irrepressible Tara Morris for infusing the photo shoots and the photos with her energy and detail-seeking eye. Many family, friends, and colleagues offered their support, inspiration, and recipe-testing and/or tasting services. Thank you all—family members, food friends, college friends, J.P. friends, and everyone in between. Big thanks to Rachel and Alon Munzer, who offered their beachy hideaway so I could "finish" my manuscript. A lifesaver! My husband Galen is the most thoughtful and steadfast sounding board and morale coach, ever. Thank you, my love. Finally, I am grateful every day for my funny boys, Quincy and Ellis, the fiercest critics a cook could have. Love you guys the most.

Table of Contents

WELCOME!

IF YOU'RE READING THIS, you must be interested in finding ways to keep cooking a regular part of your filled-to-the-brim life. I know I am.

I've been interested in food and cooking since I was a teenager, and I've worked with food my entire career. Over the years, home cooking has always anchored me. Whether I'm planning an elaborate dinner party, learning to break down a whole fish, or putting Tuesday's dinner on the table, I'm happiest when I'm learning about food and cooking and putting those lessons into practice. But as any working parent knows, this is easier said than done.

Before children, cooking was a choice. If I wanted to cook a three-course meal and eat it at nine o'clock on a weeknight, I did. If I wanted to skip dinner in favor of popcorn, wine, and Netflix, I did that, too. When my husband and I moved in together, we threw dinner parties, made jams and pickles, and baked cakes and pies all the time. Cooking was as much a hobby as a way to feed our family of two. Then our family doubled in size, and daily life became a much bigger balancing act that included the need to feed two small boys. Multiple times, every single day!

This need is not always a source of joy, as millions of parents will tell you (especially those who find themselves shelving their list of must-try recipes in order to make their thousandth pot of buttered noodles). But early in the current era of cooking for my young children, I decided I needed to keep the weekly chaos at bay while keeping the cooking spark lit—so I started planning our weekly meals. Since then, I've written our week's menu in plain sight on our kitchen chalkboard. This simple act has two wonderful outcomes: I'm able to manage expectations (for those who can read) and it keeps me honest.

Menu planning might sound like dowdy mom-sense, but let's get past that. Planning has made me a better cook. Carving out the time to think through the week and figure out our meals has given me the space to find new sources of inspiration, to try new dishes and techniques, and to flex my improvisational cooking muscles. When you know what you're cooking on any given night, and the ingredients are ready, waiting, and possibly prepared—you're stepping into the kitchen with an advantage. The clock might be ticking, the hangries might be setting in, but you're armed with a plan.

EVERY FAMILY IS DIFFERENT, and every person reading this cookbook will develop their own logic about menu planning. For me there are four basic tenets guiding the choices I make: economy, sustainability, creativity, and sanity.

I look for economy—how can I save time and money? I'm committed to sustainability and try to make thoughtful purchases that will support local growers and (in my own way) have a positive impact on the planet. Cooking is one of the ways I exercise my creativity. It's one of the most basic reasons I am a cook, so I want to make space for that in my life. Lastly, I do it for my sanity: life is complex—dinner doesn't have to be.

Make the Time: Like most habits, weekly home cooking requires some commitment. Every week, I try to block out time to make next week's menu plan. It might be ten minutes on the back of an envelope, or it could be an hour and a stack of new cookbooks.

Check the Calendar: What nights are we all together? What nights is one parent out? What about after-school activities or date nights? If only one parent is home, we keep it simple—soup or turnovers from the freezer; burritos or grilled cheese sandwiches. We try to sit down together for dinner at least twice a week—so those meals might have a little more effort behind them.

Check the Budget: We set a monthly budget and try our best to stick to it. It's doable if we focus mostly on plant-based meals and minimally processed or prepared foods; and when we buy meat or fish, we stretch that protein over a couple of meals.

Check the Pantry: We don't have a ton of storage space in our kitchen, so I try to keep dry goods moving through. If I see some black beans or polenta hanging around on the shelf for a while, they might end up as the starting points for a weekly plan.

Consider the Season: What's good right now? In the fall, we're eating lots of leafy greens and roasted squash. Apples, too. In the thick of winter we devour all those roots and brighten things up with a lot of citrus. Spring is all asparagus, greens, peas, and radishes. Summer—tomatoes and corn for life. I love seasonal eating: the anticipation, the abundance of certain foods yielding to the next season's standouts. I'm no purist, but seasonal flavors definitely influence our choices while helping us tune in to agriculture and its rhythms.

Brainstorm the Dishes: I've heard from a lot of people that this is the hardest part, because falling into a dinnertime rut is so easy (I do it all the time). Not to mention that predicting what your family will actually eat is similar to predicting the future. I can't say I've solved the riddle, or that my children eat everything I make—they certainly do not. But I try to strike a balance of satisfying my own needs as a cook and eater with flavors and dishes that won't totally gross out the boys. At least one or two nights of the week are fully child-friendly: we have a "white dinner" almost every week (that's buttered noodles and roasted cauliflower), as well as something everyone can customize, like tacos or rice bowls. The other nights are about exposure and variety—at least, in theory. I also plan to make at least one dish or ingredient (like a whole chicken or a batch of grains) that can be used in a few different ways over the course of the week.

Shop and Prep: Once the plan's in place, I make a list and head to the store and farmers market. We try to do that on Saturdays, so there's a breather between gathering groceries and prepping the goods. Then I think through what can be done in advance to save time and effort on weeknights and give myself a couple of hours to get it done. From there, weeknight cooking falls into place, usually in under forty minutes on a given night.

....

HOW TO USE THIS BOOK

THIS BOOK INCLUDES sixteen seasonal weekly menus with guidance about how to streamline your efforts, including which dishes are easy to double and freeze—making life easier down the road.

Every menu is designed with a couple of dishes or building blocks that can be made ahead of time. (**THESE COMPONENTS, WHEN USED AS INGREDIENTS IN OTHER RECIPES, ARE INDICATED LIKE THIS.**) Sometimes these include batch recipes; sometimes they are a variety of smaller dishes that can be pulled together quickly to create something your family will (hopefully) devour. A pot of chili might get served with quesadillas one night and ladled over baked sweet potatoes later in the week. A traditional pot roast is transformed into a pasta dish. A roasted chicken begets tortilla soup.

You can follow the menus faithfully, or you can pick a few of dishes in a given week and plug them into your own plan. Typically, the first two or three meals will give you the most bang for your buck in terms of efficiency, so if there are weeks where you won't be cooking dinner every night, this is a great place to start.

My hope is you will absorb a little of my zeal for menu planning and find, along the way, plenty of good ideas to answer the proverbial question: "What's for dinner?"

THE UPSIDE OF MENU PLANNING

Reduce Spending and Waste: When you plan out what you're cooking, you only buy and use what you need. Some experts estimate that 40 percent of food in America is wasted—along with the land and water resources used to produce that food. Food waste is a big issue with a big environmental impact, but one that families can address when they plan ahead. And since you reduce spending when you reduce waste, there's really no downside here.

Build Skills: Like any craft, the more you practice cooking, the better you get. When you cook a lot, you learn how to streamline the process, how to step away from rigidly following recipes, and how to get creative with ingredients to make things your very own. When you're purposeful about it, you can learn so much about building flavors and strengthening techniques. It's incredibly satisfying.

Take Time to Make Time: For me, spending a couple of hours in a stress-free kitchen on a Sunday is blissfully worth it. When I have a refrigerator full of prepped ingredients I know that our mid-week lingering at the park or library won't result in dinnertime chaos.

EVER SINCE I STARTED POSTING my weekly chalkboard plans to social media, people have asked me how I stay the course amidst the other priorities in our family's life. First, cooking is part of who I am—I just do it. After that, it's not magic, but here are a few strategies I've developed along the way.

Embrace the Freezer: The freezer is one of the top five most important tools in my kitchen (see also: sharp knives, cast iron skillets, dutch oven, sheet pans). It's like an extension of the fridge. I keep stuff in quick rotation—so if I make a double batch of pulled pork and freeze half, I'll add the second batch to the menu within a couple of weeks. The longer dishes stay in there, the more the freezer starts to feel like a very cold graveyard of ice-crystally items you're no longer in the mood to eat. I like to avoid that; freezing food is a huge part of the way I cook now.

I freeze almost everything in one form or another—cooked meats and grains; stock, soup, stew, and beans in their liquid; fritters, turnovers, and casseroles; cookies, cookie dough, pastry dough; some blanched and roasted vegetables; fruit; fish and fish cakes; and vegetable trimmings for making flavorful stock.

There's no shame in playing freezer roulette on a regular basis—it's saved my butt on many occasions.

Pick Your Battles: I have one very picky eater in my family, but dinnertime drama discourages me, so we try not to make a big deal out of his choices. I make what I make, and often include a component to accommodate him (usually a pot of noodles). We ask Ellis to take a taste of what is being served. (He typically protests and makes a fuss.) If there's nothing at the table he'll eat, he can have toast or a banana, or make up for it in the morning. Minimizing conflict at the table helps keep morale up for doing it all over again the next day.

Try Something New: If Ellis is picky, Quincy is (sort of) adventurous. He devours bluefish, avocados, squid, and when I watch him dig into a bowl of mussels, I'm one proud mama. Point being, if we hadn't encouraged him to try different foods, we wouldn't know how much he loves mussels (or sardines, for that matter). I expose my kids to new things over and over, and even though I'm not always successful, every dinner fail is worth it to find these hidden winners.

Key Word: Flexible. I can't tell you how many times I've made a weekly plan only to veer off course, or when I've gotten so disorganized I haven't thought through meals at all. When plans run amok or don't exist, I rely on improvisation and whatever the fridge and pantry hold to carry me through. The only rule I follow is to not let food go to waste. Fried rice, frittata, pizza, loaded toast, baked potatoes, and grain bowls are all good ways to use up what's in the fridge when you're at loose ends for dinner.

ABOUT THE INGREDIENTS

PEOPLE MAKE ALL KINDS OF CALCULATIONS when deciding what to feed their families. Often it has to do with how much food costs and how long it takes to prepare, but sometimes, too, with how the food was grown or raised, how far it traveled, and so forth. It's a tricky topic—everyone's priorities (and food budgets) are different, so rather than tell you what to buy, I'll just share what makes sense for my family.

Picky about Proteins: These days, animal proteins are more like really great supporting cast members, rather than starring roles, on our dinner plates. We eat meat, but we are pretty picky about it. We aim for it to be antibiotic free and raised in a humane way. I buy most of our meat from a Vermont-based CSA-style service, so I can learn a little about the producers and how they operate their farms. This means we spend more on meat, so often we go for cheaper cuts and make them count by preparing them carefully, shrinking the portion sizes, and stretching the meat across a couple of meals.

When it comes to fish, I try to stick to wild-caught domestic species, in season. (And if it's caught in New England waters, even better.) Fresh fish is something we eat occasionally—once a month, maybe (except in summer when it's more like two or three times a month, at least). Though I love to splurge on wild-caught salmon, bringing home lesser-appreciated species such as bluefish, mackerel, and redfish, along with farmed shellfish, is a great way to experiment and keep costs down.

What's in Season? I talk about my loyalty to seasonal produce throughout the book—it's where my buying decisions begin. I try to consistently support small-scale farms and farmers by setting aside a portion of our budget every week, year-round, to buy food produced in New England. In the winter, that portion is smaller; in summer, it swells. I pay attention to prices when local foods come into season—there are often really good deals to be had when apples or asparagus are super-abundant, for example.

Stocking the Pantry: A well-stocked pantry makes cooking easier, especially on the nights when you're putting dinner together on the fly. In my kitchen, there's not a ton of storage space, so I don't keep things in multiples or in great volume. But here's what I try to always have on hand:

- **Oils:** I cook almost everything in olive oil, unless I'm deep-frying (which is rare) or cooking on really high heat—in which case, I also keep a neutral oil with a high smoke point, like canola or safflower. I like having sesame oil around to finish some dishes, and occasionally I'll splurge on a fancy walnut or almond oil. I squirrel away my bacon fat in a little Mason jar, which comes in handy for high-heat searing.

- **Aromatics and herbs:** For starting or enhancing most things we cook: yellow and red onions, garlic, ginger, carrots, shallots, parsley, and often cilantro.

- **Nuts and nut butters:** I keep nuts and nut butters around for snacking, baking, and sprinkling onto salads and vegetable dishes; puréeing into sauces, smoothies, and so forth. The usual suspects include peanut butter, tahini, walnuts, almonds, and sesame and pumpkin seeds (the latter is excellent in pesto).

- **Grains and starches:** A minimum of two or three types of pasta (for our noodle monster), coarse cornmeal, basmati and brown rice, oats, barley, all-purpose flour, a potato of some kind, and a loaf of crusty, grainy bread.

- **Beans:** My favorite category of food! I always have chickpeas (canned and dried), black beans, and French lentils (which cook quickly, so are nice in a pinch). Often I have pintos, cannellini, and red lentils, too.

- **Sweeteners:** Honey, maple syrup, granulated sugar, molasses (which I use on its own and to mix into white sugar to create brown sugar).

- **Dairy:** Whole milk plain yogurt, unsalted butter, Parmigiano-Reggiano cheese, cheddar cheese (mostly for snacking, but also for stovetop mac-and-cheese, quesadillas, grilled cheese, and the like), and usually ricotta.

- **Sources of acidity:** These are vital. Acids are essential to balancing everything from salad dressings to stews. I keep about three or four vinegars, including red wine, apple cider, rice wine, and balsamic (plus an occasional splurge on something fancy). Lemons? Always! Lemons, salt, and olive oil are like a holy trinity of simple home cooking.

- **Liquids:** Whole peeled tomatoes in their juice, coconut milk, and (homemade) chicken stock.

- **Additional sources of flavor:** Anchovies, soy sauce, hot sauce, dijon mustard, a few different types of salt. (As I write this I have Kosher, flaky sea salt from England, and hickory-smoked salt.) I also have a modest but impactful collection of spices on hand.

- **Eggs:** They're so important they have their own category! I have those, too.

....

This is a sturdy pantry that can be a jumping-off point for your weekly plans, while also delivering some pretty good meals if you're in a pinch or feel like improvising instead of planning. Cycle seasonal produce and quality meats through your kitchen, along with the occasional specialty item, and you're good to go!

Ok—enough guidelines. Let's cook dinner.

January

CLASSIC ROAST CHICKEN • ROASTED POTATOES

TORTILLA SOUP

NORI ROLLS • MISO SOUP

STIR FRY

AFTER YEARS OF THROWING MODERATION TO THE DOGS in December and repenting in January, I've recently resolved to try something different: no New Year's diets. This means general moderation all year long and maintaining balance through the holiday season. Whether it happens or not, I just carry on as usual in the New Year—a time when I'm moved to embrace post-holiday lightness while mixing in some homey cold-weather dishes. That's where this menu lands.

THIS MENU STARTS with a whole roast chicken (a building block for future meals if ever there was one) and transforms the carcass and any remaining meat into a warming, reviving soup with the power to win kids over.

Plan to salt the bird the night before and leave the chicken in the fridge uncovered overnight, giving the skin a chance to dry out, which helps it get crispier during cooking (if you don't have time, salt it thirty minutes ahead instead and pat the meat dry before cooking).

While the bird cooks, you'll have time for some prep for the week and to get the ingredients ready for the Cilantro Lime Chicken Stock. After dinner is done, I toss the carcass (the backbone, neck, and breast bones) into a pot of water and get the stock started during the boys' bedtime routine. I can finish and store it before I put myself to bed for the night. And with that, our week is off to an organized start.

THE BIG COOK

SALT AND ROAST THE CHICKEN

MAKE THE CILANTRO LIME
CHICKEN STOCK

OTHER WAYS TO GET AHEAD

SLICE CARROTS FOR THE MISO SOUP

MAKE THE TOFU, CHOP BROCCOLI, AND
MAKE BROWN RICE FOR THE STIR FRY

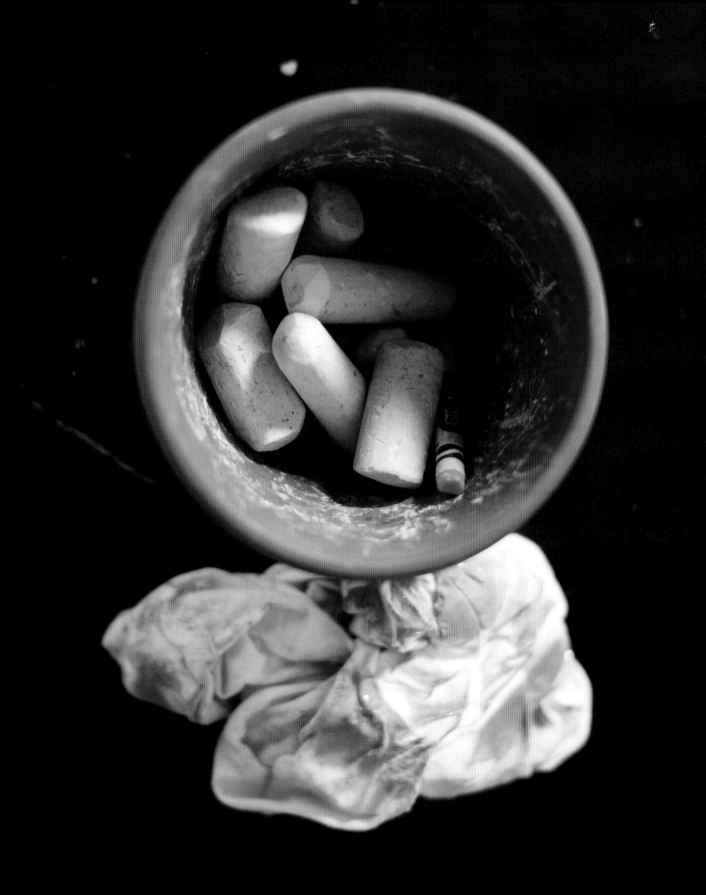

A Bird in the Hand

ROAST CHICKEN IS A DISH every cook should feel confident about. Beautiful and broadly appealing to serve to guests, but straightforward enough to make anytime. And while there are a billion recipes for it out there, this method, borrowed from the *Zuni Cafe Cookbook*, uses little more than salt and high heat to get the most from the bird (including a shorter cooking time than usual—bonus). Serve the chicken and potatoes with a simple green salad and take pleasure in the basics.

PS: The timing on the potatoes depends on their size. If you can find the 1-inch baby potatoes, they take about 40 minutes; but larger spuds cut into 1-inch pieces will be a little faster.

Classic Roast Chicken · Roasted Potatoes

30 MINUTES ACTIVE, 60 MINUTES TOTAL · *serves 4 to 6*

ROAST CHICKEN

1 3½-pound whole chicken

1 tablespoon salt

5 to 6 sprigs mixed fresh herbs (parsley, rosemary, and thyme, for example)

Freshly ground black pepper, to taste

ROASTED POTATOES

1½ pounds baby potatoes (red or yellow, the smaller the better)

1 to 2 tablespoons olive oil

¼ teaspoon salt, plus more to taste

3 to 4 sprigs rosemary

1 **Salt the chicken.** The night before cooking (or at least 30 minutes ahead), unwrap and dry the bird thoroughly with paper towels. Salt it all over (about a scant teaspoon per pound of chicken) and refrigerate, uncovered, overnight. This helps the skin dry out, which will make it crispier in the end.

2 **Roast the chicken.** Heat the oven to 475°F and place racks in the top and bottom positions. About 30 minutes before cooking, remove from the fridge and place a large cast iron skillet in the oven. Tie the herbs in a bundle with twine and place inside the bird's cavity. Sprinkle with pepper and tie the legs together if you want. Take the hot skillet out of the oven and put the chicken in the pan, breast side up. Return pan to oven.

3 **Prepare the potatoes.** If they are small enough to be roasted whole, great! If not, cut into 1-inch pieces. Toss with the olive oil, salt, and rosemary and spread out into a single layer on a baking sheet. Roast in the oven for 30 to 40 minutes (once the bird has been in for 15 minutes or so).

4 **Flip the bird.** After the chicken has been in the oven for about 25 minutes, flip it, and return to the oven. Keep an eye on the temperature; I often have to turn the oven down to 450°F if the fat starts to smoke. Roast for another 15 to 20 minutes, then flip again to crisp the breast skin for 5 to 10 more minutes.

5 **Take its temp.** If it hasn't hit 160°F yet, return to the oven for another 10 minutes or so. When the skin is bronzed and the internal temperature is 160°F at the thigh, remove chicken from oven and let it rest, loosely covered with foil, for 10 to 15 minutes before carving and serving.

6 **Check the potatoes.** When the potatoes are browned and tender, remove them from the oven and discard rosemary. Cover with foil to keep warm.

7 **Serve.** Carve the chicken. Place the carved chicken and the potatoes on a platter. Serve everything family style.

DON'T FORGET!

Reserve the leftover chicken carcass (and meat, if there's any left) for the **CILANTRO LIME CHICKEN STOCK**, *the base of the Tortilla Soup.*

Stretch it Out

THIS RECIPE FROM MY FRIEND and cooking soul sister Heather is my favorite kind of recipe—full of layered flavor but super simple and intuitive. It's also unlike many of the dishes that come to mind when I think of Heather. For years in the early 2000s, we co-hosted a holiday party where her chocolate truffles, gougères, rillettes, and other fancy snacks always took the fête right over the top.

This soup is a more rustic deal than the party dishes of yore, but it's equally fabulous in its own way. Unlike truffles and rillettes, I make this frequently. In keeping with my goal to always have vegetables on the table, I'm apt to serve it with homemade guacamole (pg. 281) and chips, of course, as well as a platter of sliced cucumbers and radishes.

CILANTRO LIME CHICKEN STOCK   MAKE AHEAD!

10 MINUTES ACTIVE, 60 MINUTES TOTAL • *Makes 2 quarts plus 2 poached chicken breasts*

I LIKE TO PULL THIS STOCK TOGETHER while cleaning up after roasting a chicken. It's pretty hands-off, and it gives the soup a big flavor boost. If you didn't roast a chicken this week, simply leave out the chicken bones—the seasoned poaching liquid still works well for the Tortilla Soup.

1 **ROAST CHICKEN CARCASS**

2 whole bone-in chicken breasts

6 to 8 garlic cloves, peeled

1 teaspoon salt

1 teaspoon whole black peppercorns

1 teaspoon whole cumin seeds

Juice of 1 lime, plus more to taste

Handful cilantro stems

1 **Start stock.** Pick the remaining meat from chicken bones and reserve. Place the bones and chicken breasts into a medium pot, cover with water by about an inch, and add garlic, salt, peppercorns, and cumin seeds, along with lime juice and cilantro stems.

2 **Bring to a simmer.** Skim off any foam that rises to the surface and poach the chicken until the meat is cooked through, about 15 to 20 minutes. Remove the chicken breasts and strain the broth, discarding solids. Taste and add more salt as needed.

3 **Reserve.** Once cool, store the stock and the poached chicken breasts in individual containers for the Tortilla Soup.

Tortilla Soup

30 MINUTES ACTIVE, 60 MINUTES TOTAL · *serves 4 to 6*

TORTILLA SOUP

2 to 3 whole dried chiles, stemmed and seeded (I like ancho—they have a warm, fruity heat)

15-ounce can whole peeled tomatoes in their juice

2 tablespoons vegetable or olive oil

1 medium white onion, cut into ¼-inch slices

3 garlic cloves, peeled

8 cups **CILANTRO LIME CHICKEN STOCK**

1 teaspoon salt

½ teaspoon dried Mexican oregano (optional)

2 POACHED CHICKEN BREASTS, shredded (reserved from Cilantro Lime Chicken Stock)

TO SERVE

Tortilla chips

Guacamole (pg. 281)

Plain yogurt or sour cream (optional)

Chopped cilantro

Lime wedges

Extra avocado slices (optional)

1 **Toast the chiles.** In a dry skillet over medium heat, toast the chiles until they become fragrant, about 1 minute on each side. Remove from heat, place in a bowl, and cover with warm water. Soak for 30 minutes, drain, and transfer to a blender along with the tomatoes.

2 **Sauté onions and garlic.** Add the oil, onions, and garlic to a medium pot over medium heat. Cook, stirring, until golden, about 7 minutes. Scoop up the onions and garlic with a slotted spoon, pressing them against the side of the pot to leave behind as much oil as possible, and add them to the blender with the chiles and tomatoes. Blend until smooth.

3 **Add the purèe to the pot.** Adjust the heat to medium-high. Cook, stirring constantly, for about 6 minutes or until the mixture has reduced to the thickness of tomato paste. Add the stock, salt, and optional oregano and stir to combine. Reduce heat to medium-low and simmer for about 15 minutes.

4 **Stir reserved chicken meat into the soup.** Simmer for a few minutes to warm it through. Taste and adjust seasoning as needed.

5 **Serve.** Ladle the soup into large bowls, then crumble a handful of tortilla chips into each bowl. Serve with garnishes alongside chips and guacamole and some sliced vegetables (goals are important).

Roll with It

YEARS AGO I WORKED AT A RESTAURANT where nori rolls were on my station. I made (and ate) them every single day. Thirteen years later, I finally recognized they make an excellent kid-friendly meal on a busy weeknight, especially when you prep in advance. (Good for breakfast, too!) Sushi rice takes less than twenty minutes, and once you get the hang of rolling, you can bang out a bunch, then teach the kiddos how.

Miso soup practically makes itself, and you can add almost anything to the broth. Mushrooms, napa cabbage, thinly sliced greens—any number of vegetables that might be hanging out in the refrigerator will work.

Nori Rolls · Miso Soup

40 MINUTES · *serves 4*

NORI ROLLS

2 cups short-grain white sushi rice (pg. 280)

2 tablespoons rice wine vinegar

1 avocado, halved and pitted

1 to 2 ounces smoked wild salmon, cut lengthwise into ½-inch strips

½ cucumber, peeled, seeded, and cut into long, thin strips

½ red pepper, trimmed and cut into long, thin strips

4 scallions, green parts only, sliced in half vertically

8 sheets nori

Salt, to taste

Pickled ginger

Soy sauce

MISO SOUP

1 large carrot, peeled and sliced into very thin coins

¼ cup thinly sliced shiitake mushrooms, stems reserved

¼ cup white miso

6 ounces firm tofu, patted dry and cut into ½-inch cubes

⅓ cup thinly sliced napa cabbage

4 to 5 scallions, green parts only, chopped

Splash of soy sauce

1 **Make the sushi rice.** When rice has absorbed all the water, turn off the heat, add 2 tablespoons rice wine vinegar, cover again, and let sit for about 10 additional minutes. Fluff with a fork and transfer to a bowl.

2 **Make the soup.** In a medium soup pot, add carrots, mushroom stems, and 6 cups of water and bring to a simmer. Simmer for about 7 minutes, until carrots are tender. (Discard the mushroom stems once carrots are cooked.)

3 **Add the miso and stir until it has dissolved.** Taste and add more miso if desired. Add the tofu and mushrooms to the soup pot and simmer for 3 to 5 minutes. Remove the miso soup from heat.

4 **Ready to roll!** Set out all of the ingredients for the rolls, including a little bowl of warm water. Place a nori sheet, shiny side down, on a clean work surface. Dip your hands in the warm water, then scoop ¼ to ⅓ cup of rice from the bowl and place it on the bottom half of the sheet. Press it out into a thin layer the same width as the nori. On the bottom third of the rice, place a horizontal line of fillings, starting with avocado and salmon, and add cucumber, peppers, and scallions. The trick is not to add too much of anything—I usually include one piece of each item— so that the nori won't be overstuffed and hard to roll.

Lift the end of the nori closest to you and roll it over the rice and filling, tucking the ends under to tighten the roll. Continue rolling until you have a long tube roughly 1-inch in diameter and an inch or so of wrapper left on each end. Dip your fingers in the water and dab the water along the wide length of the nori sheet. Continue rolling and "fasten" the dampened loose edge of the nori to the roll. Set aside, seam side down, and repeat with the next sheet of nori. Repeat until you have 8 rolls.

5 **Finish and serve.** Return the miso soup to medium-low heat and add cabbage along with the scallions. Simmer until the cabbage is tender and wilted, another 2 to 3 minutes, taste, and add soy sauce as needed. Use your sharpest knife to cut the rolls into 1-inch wheels. Arrange on a platter with pickled ginger and soy sauce; serve with miso soup.

A Better Way

AS SOMEONE WHO WENT TO COLLEGE WITH A LOT OF VEGETARIANS, I've cooked and eaten my fair share of bad stir fry. You know the type: chunky-crunchy carrots, mushy tofu, the inexplicable addition of nutritional yeast. Over the years, I've learned a few principles that have helped me get to a better place with this quick, savory, economical dish.

First, get comfortable with really high heat. Second, choose and prepare your vegetables carefully. I tend to go with one or two main vegetables and then a couple of accents. If there's one vegetable that takes longer to cook than others, I might precook it to speed things along (like the broccoli here), or thinly slice it (like carrots). Third—I picked this up from cookbook author Fuchsia Dunlop—make a quick, flavorful sauce by simmering aromatics with soy sauce until it thickens a bit, then adding honey to gloss it up.

Take these steps and stir fry will become a weeknight standby you look forward to—especially if you prep the tofu, rice, sauce, and vegetables ahead of time (you can even blanch the broccoli in advance). Getting the components ready to go early in the week will make pulling it all together a breeze.

PAN-FRIED TOFU MAKE AHEAD!

MUCH TO MY SURPRISE, tofu is one of the only foods both of my kids get reliably excited about. There are a couple of things to remember when working with it. First, the fresher, the better. If I can find nice, freshly pressed tofu, I don't season it with anything other than salt, which highlights its clean, mild flavor. Second, get it as dry as you can and be patient when searing— like other proteins, you don't want to flip it until the tofu will lift off the pan on its own. For help on how to drain and prepare tofu, see pg. 280.

6 ounces extra-firm tofu, drained

¼ to ⅓ cup neutral cooking oil, like safflower

Sprinkle of salt

1 **Slice the tofu.** Once drained, cut tofu into ½-inch cubes and transfer to a paper towel-lined colander. Pat the cubes dry one last time.

2 **Fry the tofu.** Line a cooling rack with paper towels and set aside. Place a medium cast iron skillet over medium heat. Add enough oil to fully coat the pan with a thick layer about ⅛-inch deep. When the oil is hot and shimmering, add about half of the tofu depending on the size of the pan. (Don't crowd the pan.) Cook undisturbed for 2 to 3 minutes until a crust forms on the bottom of the tofu. Lift up a piece to check the browning. When the tofu turns golden brown and lifts easily off of the pan, flip and continue cooking for an additional 2 to 3 minutes.

3 **Finish and store.** Using a slotted spoon, transfer fried tofu to the lined cooling rack. Blot away any oil and sprinkle with salt. Repeat with remaining tofu. When fully cooled, transfer to a storage container. The cooked tofu will keep in the fridge for about 5 days.

Stir Fry

30 MINUTES ACTIVE, 45 MINUTES TOTAL · *serves 4*

2 cups short-grain brown rice

Pinch of salt

½ pound broccoli florets and stalks, peeled (if needed) and cut into 1-inch pieces

3 tablespoons neutral cooking oil, like safflower

1-inch piece ginger, peeled and grated

2 to 3 scallions, chopped, white and green parts divided

2 to 3 garlic cloves, peeled and thinly sliced

1 medium red bell pepper, cut into bite-size strips

6 ounces **PAN-FRIED TOFU**

½ cup toasted unsalted peanuts, chopped

HONEY-SOY SAUCE

½ cup soy sauce

¾ cup water

1-inch piece ginger, sliced into coins

2 whole star anise

2 tablespoons honey

1 **Make the rice.** (See pg. 280 for tips.) Once rice has fully absorbed the water, turn off the heat and let sit, covered until ready to serve.

2 **Prepare the sauce.** Combine all of the ingredients, except the honey in a small saucepan, bring to a simmer over medium-low heat for 20 to 25 minutes. Strain out solids and stir in the honey. Set aside.

3 **Blanch the broccoli.** Fill a medium pot with cold water, add enough salt to make the water briny, cover, and bring to a boil. When the water is boiling, submerge the broccoli and cook until it turns bright green, about 3 minutes. Drain and plunge into cold water to stop the cooking. Pat dry.

4 **Stir fry.** Heat a wok or large skillet over high heat. When the pan is super hot, add the oil and swirl it around. When the oil shimmers, add the ginger, the white parts of the chopped scallions, and the garlic and cook, tossing and stirring, less than 1 minute. Add the broccoli and toss to combine, cook for 2 to 3 minutes, and then add the peppers and cook, tossing and stirring, for another 3 to 4 minutes. Add the tofu and the sauce (you might not need all of it) and toss to combine. Cook, stirring and tossing, until everything is hot and evenly coated.

5 **Serve.** Fluff rice with a fork and place a scoop in each bowl. Top the rice with the stir fry, then garnish with scallion greens and a handful of chopped peanuts.

> **TAKE NOTE!**
>
> *This recipe calls for a double batch of rice: 2 cups dry equals 4 cups cooked, which is more than you will need for this stir fry, but yields enough to anchor a few grown-up lunches over the course of the week. Since you're making some anyway, you might as well make extra.*

I LOVE A GOOD BAGEL, but my neighborhood in Boston didn't have a source until a few years ago. My friend Adam saw a hole in the market and ran with it. He taught himself how to bake bagels and documented his progress with each batch. He'd drop bags of bagels on friends' stoops, mine included, and gather feedback as he went. Sometimes I'd hear the doorbell and go downstairs to find half a dozen bagels waiting. It was pretty great.

Eventually, Adam made it official, opening an Exodus Bagels stall at our local farmers' market, and then finally his own shop. It's been awesome to watch it all happen. As a result of his projects, I've learned that bagels are good for any meal. Here are some ways we use them.

- **Freeze your bagels!** This seems obvious, but I'm putting it out there anyway. Slice bagels in half and store them in the freezer. They'll keep for weeks, and when you want to toast one or even thaw one to gnaw on untoasted (an Ellis specialty), a frozen bagel is much easier to deal with when sliced. I sometimes serve bagels and cream cheese for dinner with a green salad alongside.

- **Bagel sandwiches!** At Exodus, they put all kinds of crazy stuff inside the bagels—lobster salad, pot roast, you name it. I like to leave that fanciness to the pros. Instead, I start with a flavored cream cheese (I stir some horseradish and chopped scallion, lemon zest and capers, or even cinnamon and honey into the store-bought plain variety) and then add sliced cucumbers, sliced radishes, pickled onions, smoked salmon, fried eggs, avocado, roasted vegetables... you get the idea. The one thing I'd argue is that bagel sandwiches don't really need anything too crisp inside. The bagel crust gets that done.

- **Pizza bagels!** I think I love these more than my kids do. For them, it's a strange hybrid, but for me, it's a super-fun, super-fast meal with a little novelty thrown in. I lightly toast four bagels and top each half with about an ounce of pizza sauce. Toppings go next: a couple slices of pepperoni per half bagel or a little handful of thinly sliced mushrooms. Shred some mozzarella and sprinkle it on there, maybe adding a few pinches of finely grated parmesan. Next, line a baking sheet with parchment paper, put the bagels on the sheet, and place under the broiler for two minutes or so, watching carefully so the pizzas don't burn. When the cheese is browned and bubbly, remove the sheet pan from the oven and garnish the pizzas with torn basil leaves, if that's permissible in your family. (Only grownups go for basil in ours. Sigh.)

- **Bagel chips!** Slice a thawed bagel into thin chips, toss with olive oil and salt, and bake in a 375°F oven until browned and crisp, seven to eight minutes. Cool and serve with hummus or more of that tasty flavored cream cheese.

February

CIDER-BRAISED POT ROAST • SAUTÉED GREENS • APPLE-CARROT SLAW

PAPPARDELLE WITH BRAISED BEEF

WHITE BEAN SOUP WITH SAUSAGE & SWISS CHARD

RED LENTIL SOUP • NAAN

BROWN RICE BOWLS WITH PAN-FRIED TOFU AND PEANUT SAUCE

FEBRUARY IS STILL THE DREARY DEAD OF WINTER, but between Valentine's Day, Quincy's birthday, and a week of school vacation, there are enough bright spots to give the month some bounce. That goes for the kitchen, too. We're all about the soups and braises this time of year, but by February, we're seeking light wherever we can get it. Dinners often feature ginger, yogurt, cilantro, lots of lime juice—anything that perks up the palate. In a few months that might be rhubarb and spring greens from the market, but right now I'm making it work with lots of bitter, spicy, sour, bright flavors—wherever they come from.

CHILLY WEATHER CALLS FOR COOKING HUNKS OF MEAT low and slow. The more I braise meat, the more I appreciate this method. It's adaptable (if you don't have cider, use red wine) and forgiving—you can turn the oven temperature down if you want to head out for the afternoon and the braise will probably thank you for it.

Mostly, I appreciate how these cuts of meat (and their sauces) lend themselves well to being treated like a condiment or side dish rather than the main event. This is how I like to eat meat—it's less about tucking into a big prime cut than it is about savoring the rich accents these thriftier bits bring to a meal. It leaves space to crowd more vegetables onto the plate and to stretch that richness out over the course of a couple of meals.

From start to finish, prep will take you about three to four hours this week, but you won't be standing at the stove the whole time. Thoughtful sequencing for these longer cooking sessions will save you a pile of time later in the week. Braises and pot roasts are good for that.

Here's how I handle things: I get the roast in the oven first. Once it's cooking, it doesn't need much attention. Then I start the white bean soup. While the beef and soup are doing their thing, I make the dough for naan. (I like to get my kids in on this one—punching dough, instead of one another, is good for everyone.) The last thing to cross off the list is the curry paste.

If you have time and want to get even further ahead, prep the vegetables for the rice bowls. You can also drain and pan-fry the tofu, but only if you're really in the zone.

THE BIG COOK

BRAISE THE POT ROAST

MAKE THE WHITE BEAN SOUP

MIX TOGETHER A BATCH OF NAAN DOUGH

MAKE THE CURRY PASTE

MAKE THE PICKLED CARROTS (PG. 270)

OTHER WAYS TO GET AHEAD

MAKE THE PAN-FRIED TOFU FOR THE RICE BOWLS

Lighter + Brighter

THIS MENU PUTS THE RICH AND SAVORY BRAISED BEEF over a bed of sautéed greens, like swiss chard instead of the more traditional mashed potatoes. Alongside a bright and crunchy slaw, the meal feels more balanced to me. I may or may not convince the kids to finish their greens, but between the slaw and the beef, they'll have plenty of good stuff to eat. No judgment from me if you go the meat and potatoes route—it's a classic for a reason.

CIDER-BRAISED POT ROAST

MAKE AHEAD!

30 TO 40 MINUTES ACTIVE, 4 HOURS TOTAL · *serves 8*

THE ROAST CAN BE MADE IN ADVANCE. When it comes out of the oven, just cover and refrigerate it in the pot you made it in for up to five days. When ready to serve, simply remove it from the refrigerator and warm the meat through on medium-low.

This recipe is good for two distinct meals—and depending on your family, possibly a lunch or a small stash to save in the freezer. Read: bonus dinner!

1 4-pound boneless beef chuck

Scant tablespoon salt

2 cups apple cider

2 cups beef stock

1 tablespoon vegetable oil

4 carrots, peeled and cut into 2-inch pieces

2 yellow onions, peeled and quartered

1-inch piece ginger, sliced into coins

3 garlic cloves, unpeeled

1 teaspoon fennel seeds

1 teaspoon black peppercorns

2 bay leaves

Splash of apple cider vinegar

Salt, to taste

1 **Prep the roast.** Pat the roast dry and season with salt at least 1 day (and up to 3 days) in advance of cooking.

2 **Bring it to room temperature.** About 30 minutes before cooking, take the roast out of the refrigerator and pat it dry. Heat the oven to 300°F.

3 **Start the braising liquid.** Simmer cider and stock in a medium saucepan over medium-low heat.

4 **Sear the roast.** Add the oil to a large, heavy-bottomed pot with a lid over medium-high heat. When it shimmers, add the roast and cook without moving for about 5 minutes. Flip the meat over and cook, lowering the heat a bit if necessary, until the meat has browned, another 4 to 5 minutes. It should lift easily off the bottom of the pan.

5 **Add the vegetables and aromatics.** Place the meat on a plate and reduce the heat to medium. Add carrots, onions, and ginger and cook, stirring, for 2 to 3 minutes, scraping up the browned bits on the bottom of the pan. Add a splash of the warm cider mixture, stirring to combine. Move the vegetables to the edge of the pot and return the roast to the pot. Add the rest of the cider mixture along with the garlic, fennel seeds, peppercorns, and bay leaves and bring to a simmer.

6 **Cover and set the pot in the oven.** Cook for about 2 hours, flip the meat over, cover, and continue cooking for another 90 minutes. The meat is done when it is soft and fork-tender. Remove from oven and let it cool in the pot for at least an hour; you can use that time to make the slaw and sauté the chard (pg. 271).

7 **Once cool, remove the meat from the pot.** Wipe the fat from the meat, skim it from the top of the liquid, and discard. Strain the liquid and return to pot. Taste and adjust seasoning as needed.

8 **Shred the meat and return it to the liquid.** Keep meat warm at medium-low heat until ready to use. (Reserve 2 cups of meat in the liquid for the pappardelle later in the week.)

Cider-Braised Pot Roast · Sautéed Greens · Apple-Carrot Slaw

10 MINUTES · *serves 4*

2 carrots, peeled and shredded

2 apples, diced (try Cortlands or Honeycrisps)

Juice of ½ lemon

2 tablespoons cider vinegar

½ teaspoon salt

½ teaspoon granulated sugar

¼ cup chopped parsley

¼ cup chopped mint

4 servings **CIDER-BRAISED POT ROAST**

1 bunch swiss chard, or other greens

1 **Make slaw.** Toss the carrots, apples, and lemon juice together in a large bowl. Add the cider vinegar, salt, and sugar and toss to combine. Add the parsley and mint just before serving, then season to taste.

2 **Sauté swiss chard or other greens.** (See pg. 271 for assistance if you need it.)

3 **Serve.** Reheat the pot roast if needed. Spoon the beef and its juices over the sautéed greens. Add a serving of slaw alongside.

Pappardelle with Braised Beef

25 MINUTES · *serves 4*

A DISH LIKE THIS MAKES ME FEEL CLEVER. On nights when there's no cooking mojo going on (that happens, right?), guess what? You're already more than halfway there because the big hunk of beef you braised earlier this week is waiting to be made useful again. Cook some pasta, make a quick salad, and less than twenty minutes later, you're good to go. I like to counteract the rich pasta with a nice bit of crunch and acidity from the super simple Celery-Fennel Salad on pg. 274.

1 pound pappardelle

2 cups **CIDER-BRAISED POT ROAST** in its liquid

1 to 2 tablespoons butter

Salt, to taste

Freshly ground black pepper, to taste

Minced chives

1 **Prepare the pasta and warm the beef.** Cook the pappardelle according to package directions and reheat beef in a small saucepan over medium-low heat, partially covered.

2 **Finish the pasta.** When pasta is done cooking, drain (reserve ½ cup pasta water) and return to the pot (you might not use all the pasta tonight). With the heat on medium-low, add some of the butter and some of the pasta water and stir to combine. Keep stirring and tossing until the water and butter have emulsified and cling to the pasta. Add more butter and water as needed. Sprinkle with salt and pepper.

3 **Serve.** Pile pasta into bowls and top with a spoonful of braised beef and its sauce. Garnish with chives and some cracked pepper to taste. Serve with a salad.

Soup Days

HERE'S A SEEMINGLY SIMPLE SOUP that adds up to much more than the sum of its parts. Humble celery is more than a bit player here; I love the taste alongside the beans and greens. This recipe calls for canned beans to save a little time and effort, but if you want to cook the beans from dry, go for it. When I make this soup ahead of time, I wait to add the chard and sausage until right before serving, keeping the chard's color and flavor bright. Oh, and if you haven't yet tried the old parm-rind-in-the-soup-pot trick, now's the time: it adds an extra savory oomph that completes this dish. I like to serve this meal with a pile of crostini on the side.

WHITE BEAN SOUP
WITH SAUSAGE & SWISS CHARD

MAKE AHEAD!

30 MINUTES ACTIVE, 90 MINUTES TOTAL · *serves 6 to 8*

3 tablespoons olive oil, divided, plus more for garnish

1 medium onion, chopped

3 to 4 garlic cloves, peeled and chopped

3 large celery stalks, chopped

½ medium fennel bulb, chopped

½ teaspoon salt, plus more to taste

4 to 6 cups chicken stock or water

2 bay leaves

1 sprig sage (3 to 4 leaves per stem)

28-ounce can whole peeled tomatoes in their juice

2 15-ounce cans white beans (or about 4 cups dried beans)

1 parmesan rind (optional)

1 bunch swiss chard, thick stems removed, leaves chopped

½ pound precooked sweet Italian sausages (about 2), cut into ½-inch pieces

TO SERVE

Splash of red wine vinegar

Olive oil

¼ cup shaved parmesan cheese

Chopped parsley

Red pepper flakes

Crostini (pg. 280)

1 **Sauté the vegetables.** Add the olive oil to a large, heavy-bottomed pot over medium heat. When the oil is warm, add the onions and cook, stirring, for 2 to 3 minutes. Add the garlic, celery, fennel, and a pinch of salt and cook, stirring until the vegetables have softened, about 5 to 7 minutes. Add the tomatoes and their juice, crushing them with your hands as you add them to the pot. Add salt and stir to combine all ingredients.

2 **Add the stock, bay leaves, and sage.** Increase the heat to medium-high and bring just to a boil. Reduce heat to medium and simmer, uncovered, skimming any foam that rises to the surface. Add the beans and the parmesan rind and simmer for 50 to 60 minutes, until the broth has thickened. Discard bay and sage. Add the chard and sausage to the soup and simmer another 10 minutes or so, until the chard has cooked down and the sausage is warmed through. Taste and adjust seasoning. (If saving this soup for another night, cool before transferring to a storage container and refrigerating.)

3 **Finish and serve.** Add the vinegar to the soup. Taste and adjust as needed. Ladle the soup into bowls and add a drizzle of olive oil. Finish with a few shavings of parmesan, a sprinkle of chopped parsley or celery leaves, and some red pepper flakes, if desired. Serve with crostini.

Spice it Up

I LOVE MAKING THIS RED LENTIL SOUP. It's a nice, hearty weeknight dish made from inexpensive ingredients; plus it cooks up quickly and freezes well. The flavors are bright and complex but it's so simple to put together, I feel like I'm getting away with something. Make the curry paste and naan dough ahead of time and the rest of the meal comes together easily. Make a double batch for a second dinner down the road or pack some up and bring to a friend or neighbor.

CURRY PASTE   MAKE AHEAD!

20 MINUTES · *makes about 1 cup*

TRY YOUR HAND AT MAKING CURRY PASTE once and you'll see that it's worth adding to your arsenal. You can tinker with the ingredients to emphasize your own preferences (and the odds and ends in your pantry, refrigerator, and spice drawer). This recipe is a riff off of one I found on Heidi Swanson's website, 101 Cookbooks. It's a great way to add brightness and depth to soups and stews, but try rubbing it onto chicken or fish before roasting, too.

If you've never worked with lemongrass, you want just the tender inner bulb. Cut off the root end and the tough tail—this will leave you with about a 4-inch piece that is pale yellowish white. Remove the outer layer and thinly slice the remaining piece. Freeze the trimmings for the next time you make a Vietnamese or Thai-inspired stock.

This mix will keep for about a week in the refrigerator, or you can freeze it in portions in ice cube trays to use as needed.

4 lemongrass stalks, trimmed

1 tablespoon coriander seeds, toasted and cooled

1-inch piece fresh turmeric, peeled and cut into thick chunks (or 1 tablespoon ground)

3-inch piece fresh ginger, peeled and cut into thick chunks

4 garlic cloves, peeled

2 shallots, peeled

1 hot chile pepper, quartered and seeded (red adds nice color)

¼ cup coconut oil, melted and cooled

Juice and zest of one lime

Salt, to taste

Get out the food processor. Add the lemongrass and pulse until it starts to break down. Add the coriander seeds, turmeric, ginger, garlic, shallots, and chile and pulse until the mixture forms a rough paste. Add the oil in a slow stream and mix until mostly smooth and well combined. Transfer to a bowl. Add the lime zest and lime juice. Taste and adjust as needed.

NAAN

20 MINUTES ACTIVE, 1¼ HOURS TOTAL · *serves 4*

THIS FLATBREAD RECIPE IS SIMPLE TO MAKE and a good reminder not to be intimidated by yeast. It takes an hour to rise, but it keeps well in the fridge—so make it ahead and you'll feel triumphant when dinnertime strikes later in the week. (Don't forget, store-bought naan is always there for you.)

1½ teaspoons granulated sugar

2 tablespoons warm water

½ teaspoon active dry yeast

2 cups all-purpose flour

¼ teaspoon salt, plus more for seasoning bread

½ teaspoon baking soda

1 teaspoon baking powder

⅓ cup warm milk

½ cup whole milk plain yogurt

3 tablespoons unsalted butter (for pan-frying the naan)

1 **Activate the yeast.** In a medium bowl, dissolve sugar in the water. Once dissolved, stir in yeast and let sit 10 minutes or until foamy.

2 **Mix the dry ingredients.** In a separate bowl, mix the flour, salt, baking soda, and baking powder.

3 **Mix the wet ingredients.** Add milk and yogurt to the yeast mixture. Stir to combine. Make a well in the dry ingredients in the second bowl and add wet ingredients. Mix gently until a sticky dough forms. Shape into a ball, cover bowl with a kitchen towel, and place in a warm, draft-free spot to rise for an hour or until doubled in size.

4 **Shape the naan.** Heat the oven to 200°F. Turn dough out onto a floured surface and divide into 4 equal pieces. Using a rolling pin, shape each piece into a 7-inch-long oval. Melt the butter and brush the tops.

5 **Fry the naan.** Heat a cast iron skillet over medium-high heat. Place naan, buttered side down, into the pan and, working quickly, brush the top side with butter. Cover pan, reduce heat to medium, and cook for 2 to 3 minutes or until dough begins to bubble and stiffen. Flip, salt the cooked side, cover the pan again, and cook for an additional 1 to 2 minutes. Transfer naan to a rimmed baking sheet, salt remaining side, and place in oven. Repeat with remaining dough. Keep warm in the oven until ready to serve.

Red Lentil Soup · Naan

45 MINUTES · *serves 4*

1 tablespoon plus one teaspoon coconut oil

6 tablespoons **CURRY PASTE**, divided

3 cups red lentils

10 cups stock or water

1 teaspoon neutral oil, like grapeseed or safflower

2 teaspoons black mustard seeds

4 cups baby spinach, fresh or frozen

1 teaspoon salt, plus more to taste

Lime wedges, for serving

NAAN

1 **Warm the oil.** Add the coconut oil to a large, heavy-bottomed pot (I use my 3-quart dutch oven) over medium heat. When warm, add 4 tablespoons of the curry paste and cook, stirring, for about 3 minutes.

2 **Add the lentils.** Stir, coating them in the curry paste. Cover with stock or water, bring to a boil, and then reduce to a simmer over medium-low heat. Skim any foam that rises to the surface. Simmer for 30 to 35 minutes, stirring occasionally, until the lentils are completely cooked and the soup has thickened (you may need a bit more stock or water to get the consistency to your liking).

3 **Finish the soup.** Place the neutral oil in a small skillet over medium heat. When warm, add the mustard seeds and cook for 2 to 3 minutes, stirring occasionally, until the seeds start popping. When they're done, stir the seeds and the oil into the soup. Stir in the remaining curry paste, add the spinach, and simmer for another 5 to 10 minutes, tasting and adjusting the seasoning.

4 **Serve.** Ladle soup into individual bowls and provide lime wedges and naan on the side.

Really Nice Brown Rice

DESPITE ITS REPUTATION as a dusty health food item, brown rice serves our household well. I use short-grain, which has a mildly nutty flavor and tender chew. I usually make a double batch early in the week—it takes close to an hour to cook, a little long for night-of preparation, but it keeps well in the fridge and reheats with ease (I add a splash of chicken stock before reheating to keep it soft and boost the flavor). That gives us more than enough for two family dinners, a couple of lunches, and a snack here and there. Talk about bang for your buck.

This rice dish is a simple, satisfying little supper. The zippy peanut sauce recipe makes about a cup, so you can use whatever's left for lunches or as a dip for pre-dinner vegetable snacking. It takes less than ten minutes to make, but if you do it ahead, that's one less thing to think about during dinner prep. You can also prep the pan-fried tofu ahead of time, but it is simple enough to do right before dinner if you can't get to it.

The garnishes are suggestions—if you have greens on hand that need to get eaten or red peppers you could slice up, go for it. I like to have something crunchy (radishes), something cool (cucumbers), something pickled (carrots, in this case), and an onion-y bite. But that's just me—the nice thing about bowls like this is that everyone can make them the way they like.

Brown Rice Bowls with Pan-fried Tofu and Peanut Sauce

45 MINUTES · *serves 4*

2 cups short-grain brown rice
(pg. 280)

Pinch of salt

6 ounces firm tofu, drained
(pg. 280 for instructions)

Neutral cooking oil, like canola
or safflower

PEANUT SAUCE

1 small garlic clove, peeled
and minced

Pinch of salt

1-inch piece ginger, peeled
and grated

½ cup peanut butter (smooth is
preferable, but use whatever
you have on hand)

⅓ cup warm water

1 tablespoon soy sauce, plus more
to taste

1 teaspoon brown sugar

1 teaspoon fish sauce

½ teaspoon red pepper flakes

½ teaspoon lime juice

GARNISHES

2 to 3 radishes, thinly sliced

1 small cucumber, peeled, seeded,
and sliced

¼ cup cilantro leaves, stems
removed

2 scallions, green parts
only, chopped

PICKLED CARROTS (pg. 270)

Hot sauce

1 **Start the rice.** Once rice has fully absorbed the water, turn off the heat, fluff with a fork, and let sit, covered until ready to serve.

2 **Slice the tofu.** Slice drained tofu into ½-inch cubes and transfer to a paper towel-lined colander. Pat the cubes dry one last time.

3 **Fry the tofu.** Line a cooling rack with paper towels and set aside. Place a medium cast iron skillet over medium heat. Add enough oil to fully coat the pan with a thick layer about ⅛-inch deep. When the oil is hot and shimmering, add about half of the tofu depending on the size of the pan. (Don't crowd the pan.) Cook undisturbed for 2 to 3 minutes until a crust forms on the bottom. Lift up a piece to check the browning. When the tofu turns a golden brown and lifts easily off of the pan, flip and continue cooking for an additional 2 to 3 minutes.

4 **Finish the tofu.** Using a slotted spoon, transfer fried tofu to the lined cooling rack. Blot away oil and sprinkle with salt. Repeat with remaining tofu. (If you're making this ahead, allow the tofu to fully cool, then transfer to a storage container. It will keep in the fridge for about 5 days.)

5 **Make the peanut sauce.** Mash the garlic and a pinch of salt with the side of a knife until it forms a paste. Place in a small bowl with the grated ginger and the peanut butter. Whisk in the water until combined. Add the remaining ingredients and stir until blended. Thin with a little more water if needed. Taste and adjust flavor with a splash more soy sauce or lime juice.

6 **Serve.** Place a spoonful of peanut sauce in the bottom of each bowl followed by a scoop of rice. Top with a little more peanut sauce, tofu, and garnishes of everyone's choice.

FULL OF BEANS

MOST WEEKS OF THE YEAR, I have a pot of beans on the stove. Canned beans have their place in my pantry, but they don't occupy as significant a spot as the dried ones. When Galen and I were first married and both working as freelancers, we did our best to eat well on the cheap, devising what we called "the cuisine of thrift." Beans were central to that cuisine, and we still rely on them—for good eating and to help stretch our budget.

Dried beans have been in the spotlight in recent years, which I attribute to the realization that some things you or your mom thought were hard are actually very simple. It just takes a pinch of forethought to prepare dried beans, resulting in something that's extremely delicious and fortifying—not to mention versatile.

There's some disagreement about whether you need to soak your beans, when you should salt them, how long to cook them, and so forth—but I rarely stray from my routine because it gets me the results I want: well-seasoned, delicious beans.

Here's my method: Cover with water and soak overnight. In the morning, drain, rinse, and pick out any shriveled specimens or rocks. Put them in a large saucepan (I use my dutch oven) and cover with water by one to two inches. Bring to a simmer, add whatever aromatics you want, and keep simmering on medium-low heat. I throw in a few garlic cloves, a bay leaf or two, and a dried chile—but herbs are great, as are onion and celery and fennel trimmings. (I usually check the freezer bag where I keep stock trimmings and add what makes sense.) Stir in a teaspoon or so of salt and let it simmer.

Depending on what beans or legumes you're cooking, they'll be done anywhere from thirty minutes (in the case of red lentils) to two hours (kidneys, pintos, limas, and other bigger beans with thicker skins). How do you know when your beans are cooked? Touch one. Is the shape intact but creamy and soft inside? Done! Next, taste the bean and its liquid—is it seasoned? If not, add more salt and maybe a splash of vinegar.

When they're done, portion them out. Sometimes I'll freeze half a batch in its liquid for the following week, or I'll earmark half a batch for soup and use the rest for my own simple lunches through the week. **Here are a few quick bean-based ideas:**

- **Chickpeas** tossed with olive oil, lemon juice, smoked paprika, and chopped mint. Some cucumber if I have it. Toasted pita or pita chips.

- **White beans** heated with spinach, red pepper flakes, and a drizzle of olive oil.

- **Black beans** in olive oil and lime juice with chopped avocado, pickled red onion, and cilantro. Warm corn tortilla.

- **French lentils** tossed in Grain Mustard Vinaigrette (pg. 276) with tons of chopped herbs and a chunk of baguette alongside.

March

UDON IN BEEF BROTH

BANH MI • NAPA SLAW

PENNE WITH CAULIFLOWER, GARLIC & RAISINS

STEAMED MUSSELS • CAESAR SALAD • CRUSTY BREAD

POLENTA TORTA

LIKE MANY NEW ENGLANDERS, by March, I'm *really* over it. I need to be able to leave the house without spending twenty minutes searching for hats and mittens, but we're just not there yet. However, since anyone in my family can attest that I'll also be complaining about the weather come July, I get over myself. And figure out something good to eat.

HERE AGAIN, braised meat is used as an accent rather than the focal point, giving these dinners a light feel with some added depth. So keep that in mind when portioning it. If your carnivores want more in their supper, get a larger piece of meat, scale up the recipe accordingly, and freeze what you don't use (great for future tacos, dumplings, or soups).

This menu also conjures another sort of magic: turning a purposefully mundane pasta dish into something more exciting, satisfying both the picky and the adventurous eaters at the table.

All in, it takes a mere two hands-off hours to braise the beef, so think about your sequencing and use that time to make some quick pickles and do additional vegetable prep for the week: prep the vegetables for the polenta torta, cut up the cauliflower for the pasta, shred the cabbage and carrots for the slaw, clean and dry the lettuce for the Caesar Salad. You'll be ahead of the game in no time.

THE BIG COOK

BRAISE THE BEEF

PICKLE THE VEGETABLES (PG. 270)

PREP THE VEGETABLES FOR
THE TORTA

OTHER WAYS TO GET AHEAD

SHRED THE NAPA CABBAGE AND
CARROTS FOR THE SLAW

CHOP CAULIFLOWER FOR
THE PENNE

WASH AND CHOP LETTUCE FOR THE
CAESAR SALAD

MAKE THE TORTA, UP TO THREE
DAYS IN ADVANCE

Bring on the Broth

HERE'S AN OFTEN-OVERLOOKED BONUS: A braise yields a super-savory broth that will add depth to your food. Dishes like these are exactly why I keep a freezer stash of the trimmings from other ingredient prep: mushroom stems, scallion ends, fennel tops, and so forth. A cup of trimmings gives a burst of flavor to the braising liquid, plus I love getting an extra use out of items I might have composted or tossed. I'll use the liquid in the udon soup or freeze it for later just as I would chicken stock or soup.

GINGER-BRAISED BEEF

15 MINUTES ACTIVE, 2 HOURS TOTAL · *makes about 3 cups shredded beef*

2 to 2½ pounds chuck roast

½ teaspoon salt

1 to 2 tablespoons neutral oil, like canola or safflower

2-inch piece fresh ginger, thinly sliced

2 garlic cloves, peeled

1 heaping cup assorted vegetable trimmings (onions, scallions, mushroom stems, cilantro stems, leeks, etc.)

4 cups beef stock

3 to 4 whole star anise

1 **Cube and season the beef.** The night before you braise the beef, cut it into 2-inch pieces and sprinkle with salt on both sides. (If you missed this step, salt the beef at least an hour before braising.)

2 **Braise.** About 15 minutes before cooking, remove the meat from the refrigerator. Add the oil to a large, heavy-bottomed pot (I use my dutch oven) over medium-high heat. When the oil is warm, add the beef and brown it for 2 to 3 minutes on each side.

3 **Add the aromatics.** Transfer beef to a plate and add the ginger, garlic, and trimmings to the pot. Cook, stirring, for 1 to 2 minutes, then add a splash of stock and stir, scraping the bottom of the pot to loosen the browned bits.

4 **Return the beef to the pot.** Add just enough stock to cover the meat along with a pinch of salt, and bring to a simmer. Add the star anise. Partially cover the pot (just leave the lid slightly ajar) and simmer over low heat until the beef is tender and pulls apart easily with a fork, about 2 hours.

5 **Finish.** Remove beef from the pot. Strain the liquid, discarding the solids. Shred the beef. Store in the strained braising liquid until you're ready to use it.

Udon in Beef Broth

30 MINUTES · *serves 4 to 6*

1½ cups **GINGER-BRAISED BEEF** (pg. 55) in its cooking liquid

4 cups beef broth

1-inch piece ginger, sliced into thin coins

3 to 4 whole star anise

1 cup shiitake mushrooms, stemmed and thinly sliced

2 heads bok choy, halved and thinly sliced

Soy sauce, to taste

Fish sauce, to taste

1 package udon noodles

GARNISHES

2 radishes, thinly sliced

3 to 4 scallions, green parts only, chopped

¼ cup cilantro leaves

Sesame oil, for drizzling

Hot sauce

1 **Reheat the beef if needed.** In a medium saucepan, bring the braised beef and its liquid, beef broth, ginger, and star anise to a simmer. Simmer for 10 to 15 minutes and then discard the ginger and anise. Add the mushrooms and bok choy and simmer for another 10 to 15 minutes. Taste and add soy and fish sauce as needed.

2 **Cook the udon according to package directions.** Divide the noodles into four deep bowls (you'll have extra noodles). Ladle the broth into the bowls, making sure each gets beef, mushrooms, and greens.

3 **Serve.** I like to put out little bowls of radishes, scallions, and cilantro for people to make the bowls their own. I add a drizzle of sesame oil and a few shakes of hot sauce to mine.

> **TIP!**
>
> *Toss those mushroom stems in a freezer bag and store them to flavor future stock. (This works with all your trimmings.)*

Banh Mi · Napa Slaw

30 MINUTES · *serves 4*

I HAVE THREE WORDS FOR YOU: sandwiches for dinner. Once you incorporate this one into your rotation, you're likely to keep it there. Our take on the Vietnamese sandwich, the Banh Mi, is one we re-visit all year long. Next time you have a hankering, meatballs (pg. 256), pâté, or pulled pork (pg. 241) would all be equally delicious here, too. Stumped by what to do with your extra napa cabbage? It wilts beautifully in soups or in rice or noodle dishes.

NAPA SLAW

¼ cup rice wine vinegar

½ teaspoon honey

½ teaspoon grated fresh ginger

½ cup neutral oil, like safflower or canola

½ teaspoon sesame oil

¼ teaspoon salt, plus more to taste

2 cups shredded napa cabbage
  (about ½ a small head)

1 cup shredded carrots (about 3 carrots)

3 to 4 scallions, green parts only, chopped

½ cup chopped cilantro

Thinly sliced cucumbers, red bell
  peppers, or radish

¼ cup roasted, unsalted peanuts

BANH MI

¼ cup mayonnaise

Sriracha, to taste

Fish sauce, to taste

1 baguette (around 24 inches), split in
  half vertically and cut into 4 pieces

1½ cups **GINGER-BRAISED BEEF** (pg. 55),
  shredded

1 cup **ASSORTED PICKLED VEGETABLES** (pg. 270)

1 cucumber, peeled and cut into long,
  thin slices

Scallion greens, cut into long, thin strips

Cilantro leaves, stems removed

1 **Make the dressing.** In a small jar with a lid, add the vinegar, honey, and ginger and shake until combined. Slowly drizzle in the oils, add the salt, cover, and shake until the mixture is fully blended and emulsified. Taste and adjust seasoning.

2 **Assemble the slaw.** In a large bowl, combine the cabbage, carrots, scallions, and cilantro. Add the dressing and mix to combine. Just before serving, add the peanuts.

3 **Make the sauce.** Mix the mayonnaise and sriracha to taste and add a splash of fish sauce. Taste and adjust to your liking. (I usually make this pretty mild for the gang and then add more sriracha and pickled hot peppers to my own sandwich.)

4 **Build the sandwiches.** Spread the sauce onto the sliced baguette. Layer on the braised beef, pickled vegetables, cucumber, scallions, and cilantro.

Penne with Cauliflower, Garlic & Raisins

30 MINUTES · *serves 4*

IN MY YOUNGER SON, I have an exceptionally choosy eater. It's hard to predict what he will and won't eat. We know the following: he could live on buttered noodles and, if we let him, he'll destroy a head of cauliflower on his own. So on Wednesday nights, we often indulge Ellis' tastes and have "white dinner," buttered noodles and roasted cauliflower (maybe chicken if we need a little something extra). To keep the rest of us interested, I'll combine these basics with a few ingredients from the pantry. The result is a dish that is equally quick and easy but far more intriguing.

1 head cauliflower, cored and cut into ½-inch pieces

2 to 3 tablespoons olive oil, divided

Salt, to taste

1 pound penne

2 garlic cloves, peeled and minced

¼ cup raisins or dried currants

Juice and zest of one lemon

2 to 3 tablespoons unsalted butter

½ cup toasted walnuts, chopped

⅓ cup chopped flat-leaf parsley

Freshly ground black pepper, to taste

1 **Roast the cauliflower.** Heat the oven to 425°F. Spread the cauliflower on a rimmed baking sheet and sprinkle with 2 tablespoons of olive oil and salt. Toss to coat the cauliflower. Roast for about 20 minutes, tossing once or twice, until the cauliflower is browned to your liking.

2 **Cook the pasta.** Once the penne is al dente, drain it (reserve ½ cup of pasta water) and toss with a drizzle of olive oil to coat.

3 **Start the sauce.** In a large saucepan, heat remaining olive oil over medium-low heat. Add the garlic and the raisins, along with a sprinkle of salt, and cook, stirring, for about 1 minute. Add the lemon juice and zest and cook, stirring, for 1 more minute.

4 **Add the pasta to the saucepan.** Increase heat to medium and cook, stirring to coat the pasta, for a minute or 2. Add a drizzle of pasta water and a knob of butter as you go to create a sauce that clings to the noodles. Keep warm over low heat, stirring occasionally, until the cauliflower is done roasting.

5 **Finish the pasta.** Add the roasted cauliflower, walnuts, and another knob of butter to the pan and stir to combine. Continue stirring and tossing the pasta, adding a drizzle of pasta water as needed to keep things silky, for another minute. Stir in the parsley.

6 **Serve.** Transfer to a serving bowl, then add a sprinkle of salt and freshly ground black pepper.

MUSSELS FALL INTO A SPECIAL CATEGORY OF SEAFOOD—they're filter feeders, which means they clean the water around them as they eat, making them an extra-good choice on the sustainability scale. They're inexpensive, easy to prepare, and super versatile. Mildly briny, they take well to plenty of different flavors: fennel and Pernod (one of my favorites); beer and loads of garlic; ginger and coconut milk. Plus, around here, I have to fight my older son for them—I consider this a good thing. Mussels, you win!

When I make this meal, I use part of a loaf of crusty bread to make croutons for the salad. The rest gets warmed up and dunked in the mussel broth.

And the salad! It takes more effort than your average weeknight salad, but it's worth it. I fuss over it a little, making croutons, mixing up the dressing right before I use it, washing the lettuce well and drying it completely. I also use the real deal Parmigiano-Reggiano, which makes a difference. To speed the process, I wash and dry the romaine in advance, make the dressing while the croutons are toasting, and dress the salad while the mussels are steaming.

Steamed Mussels · Caesar Salad · Crusty Bread

20 MINUTES ACTIVE, 40 MINUTES TOTAL · *serves 4*

CAESAR SALAD

1 loaf of crusty white bread, divided (1 cup cubed for croutons, the rest reserved)

1 tablespoon olive oil

Pinch of salt

1 head romaine, washed, very well dried, and torn into 1-inch pieces

Parmigiano-Reggiano, shaved, to taste

DRESSING

1 to 2 large anchovy filets

1 garlic clove, peeled

2 egg yolks

1 tablespoon lemon juice

1 teaspoon dijon mustard

½ teaspoon red wine vinegar

1 tablespoon finely grated Parmigiano-Reggiano

½ cup olive oil

Salt, to taste

Freshly ground black pepper, to taste

STEAMED MUSSELS

3 to 4 pounds mussels (1 pound per person is ample)

2 tablespoons unsalted butter, divided

1 medium onion, diced

2 to 3 garlic cloves, peeled and minced

1 hot pepper, sliced into rings (remove seeds for less heat)

¾ to 1 cup beer of your choice (I usually go with an IPA)

2 tablespoons chopped flat-leaf parsley

1 **Make the croutons.** Heat the oven to 375°F. Toss the cubed bread and olive oil together with salt in a small bowl. Transfer to a rimmed baking sheet and bake for 5 minutes, then toss or flip the croutons and bake for another 3 to 5 minutes depending on how dark you like them. Remove from the oven, but leave the oven on to warm the bread while the mussels are steaming.

2 **Make the dressing.** Mince the anchovy and garlic together with a pinch of salt and use the side of a knife to mash into a paste. Transfer to a small bowl and whisk in the egg yolks, lemon juice, mustard, vinegar, and cheese. In a slow stream, whisk in the olive oil. Stir in the salt and pepper, then taste and adjust seasoning. Set aside.

3 **Prep the mussels and warm the bread.** Place the mussels in a colander and rinse with cold water. Discard mussels with open or cracked shells. Pull off and discard any "beards," the fibrous threads that sometimes stick out from the shells. Wrap remaining bread in foil and place in the oven.

4 **Cook the mussels.** Melt 1 tablespoon of butter over medium heat in a large pot with a lid. When it foams, add the onions and cook, stirring, until they start to soften and turn translucent, 3 to 5 minutes. Add the garlic and peppers and cook, stirring, for another 2 to 3 minutes. Add the beer and mussels, turn heat up to high, and cover the pot. Steam until the mussel shells have opened, 5 to 8 minutes. Add the remaining butter and the parsley and shake the pot to combine.

5 **Finish the salad.** In a large salad bowl, toss the romaine with the dressing (you'll have extra dressing—more Caesar salads for you!). Add the croutons and toss again.

6 **Serve.** I like to bring the whole pot to the table, but you may want to transfer to a large serving bowl. Don't forget a bowl for the shells! Serve alongside the warm bread and salad.

Polenta Torta

40 MINUTES · *serves 6*

A TORTA MEANS MANY THINGS in many cultures and cuisines, but I've been making versions of this layered polenta dish, adapted from the great Paula Wolfert's *Mediterranean Grains and Greens* cookbook, for years. This sturdy meal can be made up to three days ahead, and it's especially comforting when we're transitioning into spring but haven't quite shaken off the chill. I like to serve this with a bright spinach salad tossed with Grain Mustard Vinaigrette (pg. 276).

2 tablespoons olive oil, plus more for brushing

1 cup coarse ground cornmeal

¼ teaspoon salt, plus more to taste

1 large garlic clove, peeled and minced

1 bunch swiss chard, stems and leaves divided and chopped

10 white or brown mushrooms, stemmed and roughly chopped

¼ cup chopped parsley (leaves and tender stems)

⅓ cup finely grated parmesan or pecorino, plus more for topping

1 **Prepare a baking dish.** Brush a 9x11 inch dish with olive oil.

2 **Make the polenta.** Bring 4 cups of water to a boil in a medium saucepan and add the cornmeal and the salt. Whisk until the mixture begins to bubble and thicken, then reduce heat to medium-low and cook, stirring occasionally, until the cornmeal has fully absorbed the water and is fragrant and pulling away from the sides of the pot, about 20 to 25 minutes.

3 **Sauté the vegetables.** Add the oil to a medium skillet over medium heat. When it shimmers, add the garlic and chard stems. Reduce heat to medium-low and cook until the garlic is fragrant and the chard stems have softened. Add the mushrooms, stir, and increase the heat to medium-high. Cook, stirring, for 7 to 10 minutes, until the mushrooms have collapsed, released their water, and the water has evaporated. (Bump the heat up to high toward the end if necessary.) Add the chard leaves and parsley, reduce heat to medium, and cook until the chard has wilted and its liquid has mostly evaporated. Add salt to taste.

4 **Assemble the torta.** Spread half of the polenta into the bottom of the baking dish, then add the vegetables in an even layer. Sprinkle half of the cheese over the vegetables and cover with the remaining polenta. Use a spatula to smooth it evenly over the vegetables. If storing the torta to eat later, cool and cover tightly with plastic wrap.

5 **Finish.** Heat the oven to 375°F. Sprinkle with the remaining cheese and cook in the oven for 15 to 20 minutes until the torta is heated through and the cheese is browned and bubbling.

NOTE:

If making the torta ahead, store in the refrigerator for up to 3 days. Bring to room temperature, sprinkle with remaining cheese, and bake for 35 to 40 minutes, until heated through and bubbling.

SPICE WORLD

I'M DEFINITELY A SEASONAL SPICE USER. In the warmer weather, I toss just about everything with olive oil, salt, lemon juice, and fresh herbs, but cold days send me straight to the spice drawer to add some interest to my cooking. I keep my collection stocked with versatile workhorse spices and build on that foundation when I'm exploring the flavors in a new-to-me cuisine.

For those that I use most, I keep whole spices on hand so I can toast and grind as needed. (Sometimes this step can feel insurmountable, so I store ground spices too.) But when I do grind my own—either with a mortar and pestle or an electric grinder—the added intensity of flavor is always worth the effort.

....

HERE'S WHAT'S IN MY DRAWER:

Specialty salts: I use kosher salt in my everyday cooking, but I also love experimenting with different finishing salts. I favor Maldon, a delicate, flaky sea salt; it's delightful sprinkled over every salad ever made and anything with chocolate. Recently I've also been playing around with grey sea salt (I love the briny, mineral-y crunch it lends to dishes) and smoked sea salt.

Black peppercorns: I buy these in bulk since I tend to tear through them. Whole, they're added to stocks, marinades, chai mixes, simple syrups, and so much more. Freshly ground, they add lift and bite to everything.

Ground peppers: This category is enormous! I tend to use dried ground red peppers to finish dishes so everyone gets the level of spice they can tolerate. I often have ground chipotle (smoky with just a little heat) and ground ancho (fruity and mild) in my drawer—but here are a few other favorites:

- **Aleppo:** A fruity Turkish pepper with mild-to-medium heat. My favorite for adding to rubs for grilled meat (lamb and chicken pair especially well with Aleppo), sprinkling over grilled or roasted vegetables, or stirring into a bowl of beans.

- **Red pepper flakes:** I use this all-purpose chile in brines and marinades and for finishing lots of different dishes—including anything with tomato sauce and melted cheese.

- **Smoked paprika:** This ground sweet pepper gives dishes a smoky boost. I love it dusted over chickpeas tossed with olive oil, feta, and herbs, but I use it in all manner of stews, marinades, and spice rubs, too.

Cumin: I go through more of this spice than any other. Its musky, earthy flavor works in Indian, Latin, Middle Eastern, even some Asian dishes. It can stand alone and is delightful when blended with other spices. Almost any roasted vegetable benefits from a dusting of cumin, as does most grilled, roasted, or braised meat.

Cinnamon: I use cinnamon all the time in baking, of course, but it's especially good when used in savory dishes. Blend it with cumin and red pepper flakes for lamb dishes or add a stick to a pot of black beans for a fragrant layer of flavor.

Whole nutmeg: Citrusy and nutty, nutmeg is one of my favorite flavors. I love it grated over hot cocoa or stirred into anything creamy (like pasta with cream sauce or a chicken pot pie).

Coriander: A floral flavor that adds nice balance when mixed with cumin; they're often found together in spice rubs or marinades for Latin-style dishes.

Cardamom: I love this spice; it has a anise-y kick to it, and it's great blended into a chai tea blend or masala mix. In baked goods, it's especially delicious in buttery cakes and cookies.

Sumac powder: A newer favorite, inspired by forays into the Ottolenghi cookbooks. I dust it over greens or pita chips before they go into the oven to crisp. I also use it to mix up my own batch of za'atar, a tasty all-purpose Middle Eastern seasoning.

To save space in my spice drawer, I like to make my own blends. It's fun to create new flavor combinations and to see how they can change the profile of a dish. Here are a few of my favorites:

LAVENDER + ROSEMARY + THYME

SMOKED PAPRIKA + CUMIN + CINNAMON

SMOKED SALT + SAGE + RED PEPPER FLAKES

Early April

MUSHROOM-BARLEY SOUP WITH PARSLEY PESTO •
CHEESE & BREAD

FALAFEL • CUCUMBER-RADISH SALAD

STUFFED PORTOBELLO MUSHROOMS •
BARLEY-CAULIFLOWER SALAD

RICOTTA FRITTATA WITH GREENS

FIDEOS WITH SAUSAGE AND CHICKPEAS

EARLY APRIL is a sweet but somewhat confusing time of year. The days are getting longer by the minute, the flowers and trees and grasses are starting to perk up, but we're still looking for ways to ward off the chill. Here's a menu for a week that sits in the middle of that transitional time—it's earthy and nourishing for those days when we are done with winter but the weather is not *quite* what comes to mind when we think spring.

ALTHOUGH TIME IS AT A PREMIUM ALWAYS, I never regret spending a couple of hours over the course of the weekend batch cooking a few components for meals throughout the coming week. The dinner hour becomes more about assembling and less about starting from scratch when people are tired and hungry.

This particular menu calls for a good chunk of prep work, but it won't wipe out your Sunday, especially if you're smart about sequencing.

Soak the chickpeas overnight before you make the falafel or the fideos (if you're just making fideos, canned work fine). The next day, roast some cauliflower and while that's cooking, get a batch of barley going and make the falafel mix. You could call it good there or take it a step further and make the Mushroom-Barley Soup; and/or clean the lettuce and pickle onions for falafel night.

THE BIG COOK

SOAK THE CHICKPEAS FOR THE FALAFEL AND FIDEOS

COOK HALF OF THE SOAKED CHICKPEAS FOR THE FIDEOS

MAKE A BATCH OF BARLEY

ROAST THE CAULIFLOWER

MAKE THE FALAFEL MIX

OTHER WAYS TO GET AHEAD

MAKE THE MUSHROOM-BARLEY SOUP

PICKLE THE RED ONIONS (PG. 270)

CLEAN AND DRY THE LETTUCE FOR THE CUCUMBER-RADISH SALAD

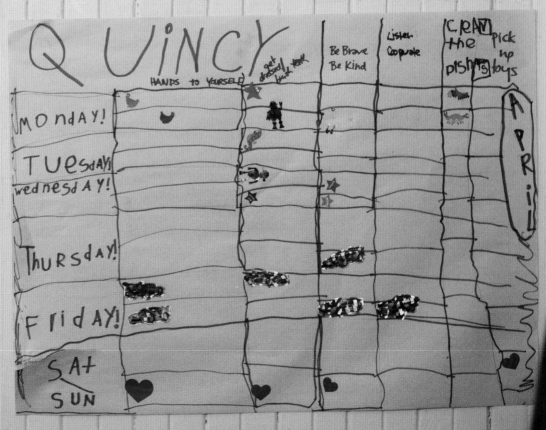

QUINCY

HANDS TO YOURSELF   get
                    dressed
                     brush
                     teeth

Be Brave   Listen   CLEAN   pick
Be Kind   Cooperate   the   up
                        DISHES toys

MONDAY!

TUESday!

wednesday!

Thursday!

Friday!

SAT

SUN

A
P
R
I
L

Elevating a Standard

THIS MEAL IS JUST THE THING on a chilly Sunday in March. Calling for only a few ingredients, the soup comes together with ease, offering up something understated and earthy. Because the soup is so simple, homemade stock makes a big difference here.

I like to serve this soup with a few upgrades: a handful of tender greens, a spoonful of bright parsley pesto, some crusty bread, and a hunk of nice cheese alongside. (Camembert, with hints of mushroom in its edible rind, pairs well.) Remember to take the cheese out of the fridge about thirty minutes before dinner to take off the chill.

A BATCH OF BARLEY

MAKE AHEAD!

5 MINUTES ACTIVE, 45 MINUTES TOTAL · *makes about 6 cups*

2 cups pearl barley

6 cups water

½ teaspoon salt

1 teaspoon olive oil

1 **Prep and cook.** Rinse the barley in a fine-mesh strainer until the water runs clear. Transfer to a medium saucepan with a lid. Add the water and the salt, bring to a boil, then reduce heat to a low simmer and cover. Cook until the barley has absorbed all of the water and is tender, about 40 minutes.

2 **Cool and store.** Line a rimmed baking sheet with parchment or a silicone liner and spread out the barley to cool. Pat it dry with a paper towel if needed. When the barley has cooled, transfer to a storage container and toss with olive oil. Refrigerate until ready to use.

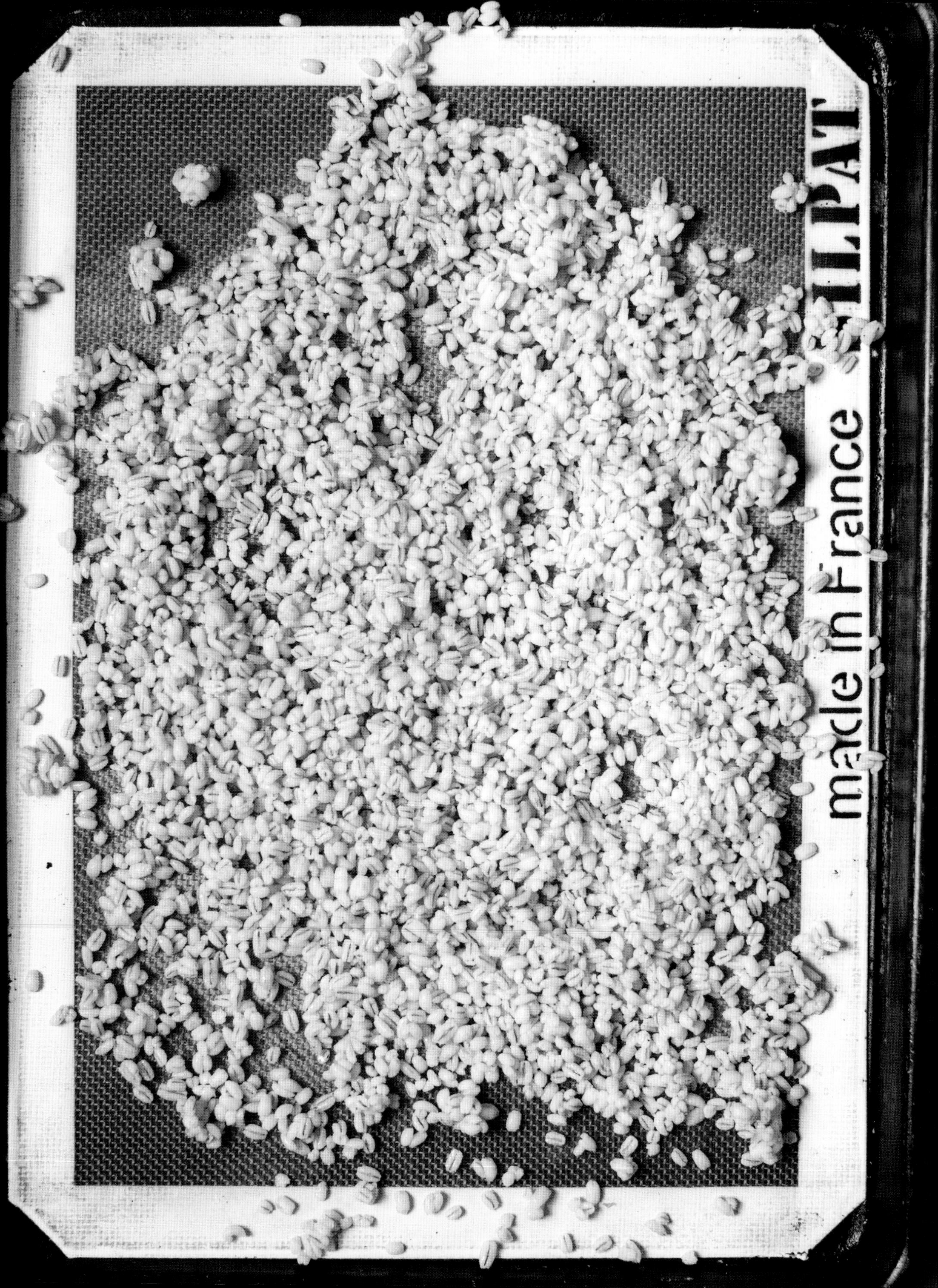
made in France

Mushroom-Barley Soup with Parsley Pesto

30 MINUTES ACTIVE, 1 HOUR TOTAL · *serves 6*

2 tablespoons olive oil

½ medium onion, chopped

2 medium carrots, peeled and chopped into ¼-inch pieces

1 tablespoon thyme leaves, chopped

1 teaspoon salt, plus more to taste

4 medium portobello mushrooms, stems removed and cut into ½-inch pieces (about 4 cups)

8 cups beef or chicken stock (preferably homemade, pg. 225)

2 cups **COOKED BARLEY**

½ teaspoon freshly ground black pepper

Big handful baby spinach leaves

Pinch of red pepper flakes (optional)

PARSLEY PESTO

2 to 3 tablespoons chopped parsley

1 small garlic clove, peeled and crushed

Pinch of salt

Olive oil, for drizzling

CHEESE & BREAD

Loaf of crusty bread

½ wheel of Camembert (or another cheese your family likes)

1 **Sauté the vegetables.** Add the oil to a medium, heavy-bottomed pot over medium heat. Add the onions and cook until they start to soften, 4 to 5 minutes. Add the carrots, thyme, and a pinch of salt and cook, stirring occasionally, for 4 to 5 minutes. Add the mushrooms and stir to combine, stirring occasionally for another 4 to 5 minutes.

When the mushrooms start to soften and release their liquid, increase the heat to medium-high and cook, stirring, until the liquid has mostly evaporated and the mushrooms are thoroughly soft and collapsed. Add the stock and bring to a boil. Reduce heat to a simmer and cook for about 30 minutes.

2 **Stir in the barley.** Simmer for another 15 minutes. Stir in the salt and pepper, taste, and adjust as needed. Keep warm until ready to serve; otherwise, allow pot to cool and store in the refrigerator.

3 **Make the pesto.** Put parsley, garlic, and salt together in a mortar and pound with a pestle. Drizzle in the olive oil and continue pounding until the mixture forms a rough paste. If you don't have a mortar and pestle, finely chop the parsley and garlic. Using the side of a knife, work in the salt and coax the mixture into a paste. Transfer to a small bowl and stir in the olive oil.

4 **Finish and serve.** Reheat the soup if needed. Add a handful of baby spinach leaves and simmer until wilted. Top each bowl of soup with a spoonful of pesto. (I also like to sprinkle red pepper flakes on mine.) Put out the cheese and bread and let them have at it.

Falafel Night

IT WASN'T UNTIL I FOLLOWED A RECIPE in Yotam Ottolenghi and Sami Tamimi's cookbook *Jerusalem* that my homemade falafel was anywhere near as good as that from my favorite local falafel shop. The trick is to soak (but not cook) the chickpeas before grinding them up with the other ingredients. The result is falafel that is lighter and springier, with a crisper exterior, than those made with the cooked legumes.

After I got the hang of the falafel, it entered our regular rotation—especially because it is so easy to make in advance. It's also a great candidate for doubling and freezing. A one pound bag of dried chickpeas gives you six cups of beans after they're soaked, so I just double the quantities of all the other ingredients below and do them in batches in the food processor. I freeze the patties individually on a parchment-lined baking sheet, then stick them in a freezer bag. When it's time to fry, just add a minute or two more on each side to the cooking time.

FALAFEL

1 HOUR, PLUS TIME FOR SOAKING THE CHICKPEAS AND CHILLING · *makes about 12 patties*

1½ cups dried chickpeas, soaked overnight (3 cups once soaked)

½ medium yellow onion, peeled and roughly chopped

2 medium garlic cloves, peeled and crushed

¼ cup packed parsley leaves

½ teaspoon ground cumin

½ teaspoon ground cinnamon

½ teaspoon ground coriander

½ teaspoon baking powder

1 tablespoon flour

1 teaspoon salt

1 egg, lightly beaten

3 to 4 tablespoons breadcrumbs

Vegetable oil, for frying

TO SERVE

4 pitas

Herby Yogurt Sauce (pg. 277)

1 cup **PICKLED RED ONIONS** (pg. 270)

Hot sauce

Cucumber-Radish Salad (pg. 78)

1 **Make the falafel mixture.** Add the chickpeas to a food processor along with the onions, garlic, and parsley. Pulse until the mixture forms a coarse paste. Transfer to a bowl and add the spices, baking powder, flour, salt, and egg. Stir to combine. If the mixture is wet, add breadcrumbs, a tablespoon at a time, to help bind the falafel. Transfer mixture to a storage container and refrigerate for 1 hour or until ready to cook. (The mixture can be made 3 to 5 days ahead.)

2 **Get ready.** Heat the oven to 200°F. Line a cooling rack with paper towels and place on a rimmed baking sheet. Form falafel mixture into 2-inch patties.

3 **Fry the falafel.** In a large skillet over medium to medium-high heat, add enough oil to coat the pan with a thick layer about ¼-inch deep. When the oil is hot and shimmering, add the patties. Work in batches to avoiding crowding.

Adjust the heat between medium and medium-high as needed to keep the oil from smoking and the patties from getting too dark. Fry until deep golden and crisp, 2 to 3 minutes per side.

4 **Transfer to the cooling rack.** Sprinkle with salt and place in the oven to keep warm. Put pita in the oven on the bottom rack. Mix together the yogurt sauce. Sprinkle falafel with salt once more before serving. Transfer pita and falafel to a platter. Serve with yogurt sauce, pickled red onions, Cucumber-Radish Salad, and hot sauce.

Cucumber-Radish Salad

3 to 4 radishes

1 small cucumber

½ head romaine lettuce

¼ cup mixed mint and parsley leaves

1 to 2 tablespoons olive oil

Juice of ½ lemon

½ teaspoon sumac powder

Salt, to taste

Freshly ground black pepper, to taste

Thinly slice the radishes. Peel the cucumber, slice it in half vertically, and scoop out the seeds with a spoon. Discard seeds and cut cucumber halves into bite-size pieces. Cut or tear the lettuce into small pieces and add it to a salad bowl with the radishes, cucumber, and herbs. Toss with olive oil, lemon juice, sumac, salt, and pepper.

Variations on a Theme

IN MY EFFORT TO INVOLVE THE KIDS MORE in meal planning (and to manage their expectations at dinnertime), we recently started theming many of our weeknight meals. This isn't something pre-mom Leigh ever would have done, but here we are. It's actually great—within the framework, which streamlines and structures my brainstorming, there's plenty of room to play. Just because it's Taco Tuesday doesn't mean you're going to eat the same taco every week, right? Well, maybe you will. I won't judge. For us, this meal is a Meatless Monday standby. I love it for all sorts of reasons but chiefly because it serves one son's unexpected love for barley and the other son's cauliflower obsession. Who knew?

ROASTED CAULIFLOWER   MAKE AHEAD!

10 MINUTES ACTIVE, 35 MINUTES TOTAL · *makes about 4 cups*

ROASTED CAULIFLOWER NEVER LASTS LONG at our table, so I always make more than I need. If you roast a whole head, you'll need about half of it for the Barley-Cauliflower Salad. Throw leftovers into your lunch salad, a frittata, your weekly tacos, or eat it straight from the fridge as a snack.

1 medium head cauliflower, cored and cut into 1-inch florets

2 tablespoons olive oil

½ teaspoon salt

Heat the oven to 425°F. Toss the cauliflower florets with the olive oil and salt and spread onto a rimmed baking sheet. Roast, tossing once or twice, until the cauliflower is tender and browned at the edges, about 20 minutes. Remove from oven, cool, and refrigerate in a storage container until ready to use.

Stuffed Portobello Mushrooms · Barley-Cauliflower Salad

45 MINUTES · *serves 4*

4 portobello mushrooms

3 tablespoons olive oil, divided

½ teaspoon salt, plus more to taste

Freshly ground black pepper, to taste

½ medium yellow onion, chopped

2 garlic cloves, peeled and chopped

1 tablespoon tomato paste

1 tablespoon chopped
   flat-leaf parsley

1 teaspoon red wine or
   sherry vinegar

¼ teaspoon smoked paprika

2 cups baby spinach,
   roughly chopped

¾ cup ricotta cheese

½ teaspoon finely grated lemon zest

1 tablespoon lemon juice

Scant ¼ cup finely grated parmesan

Scant ¼ cup breadcrumbs

BARLEY-CAULIFLOWER SALAD

2 cups cooked barley

2 tablespoons olive oil

1 teaspoon finely grated lemon zest

1 tablespoon lemon juice

1 cup peas (thawed if frozen)

¼ cup chopped parsley

¼ cup chopped mint

¼ cup chopped dill

½ head **ROASTED CAULIFLOWER**

½ cup sliced almonds, toasted

½ teaspoon salt

Red pepper flakes

1. **Roast the mushrooms.** Heat the oven to 375°F. Remove the mushroom stems, chop them, and set aside. Brush mushroom caps all over with a tablespoon of olive oil and sprinkle with salt and pepper. Place stem-side down in a large baking dish or on a rimmed baking sheet lined with parchment paper. Roast until the mushrooms soften and start to release some of their liquid, about 15 minutes. Remove from oven.

2. **Prepare the filling.** While the mushrooms are roasting, add the remaining olive oil to a skillet over medium heat. When the oil is warm and shimmering, add the onions and cook, stirring, until soft, 2 to 3 minutes. Add the garlic and cook, stirring a few times, for 1 minute. Add the tomato paste and continue to cook, stirring, for another 2 to 3 minutes. Add the chopped mushroom stems and cook, stirring, for 4 to 5 minutes. Add the parsley, vinegar, and paprika and stir to combine. Add the spinach and cook, stirring, until it has wilted, about 3 more minutes. Remove from heat.

   Place mixture in a small bowl and add the ricotta, stirring thoroughly to combine. Add the lemon zest and juice along with ½ teaspoon salt and a few grinds of pepper to taste.

3. **Stuff the mushrooms.** Flip over the mushrooms and divide the filling evenly among them. In a small bowl, toss together the parmesan, bread crumbs, and a few grinds of pepper. Sprinkle each mushroom with some of the parmesan-breadcrumb mixture. Return the mushrooms to the oven for 10 to 15 minutes, until warmed through.

4. **Make the Barley-Cauliflower Salad.** While the mushrooms are roasting, place the barley in a large bowl and toss with olive oil. Add the lemon zest and juice, peas, and herbs and toss again. Add the cauliflower and almonds. Toss one last time to combine, add the salt, taste, and adjust seasoning.

5. **Finish and serve.** To get the mushroom topping nice and crunchy, place under the broiler for about 1 minute. Right before serving, give the Barley-Cauliflower Salad a drizzle of olive oil and one last squeeze of lemon juice to brighten the flavors.

Ricotta Frittata with Greens

30 MINUTES ACTIVE, 50 MINUTES TOTAL · *serves 6*

WHEN I SIT DOWN TO PLAN A WEEK'S MENU and shopping expedition, I almost always incorporate a meal where I can use up what I have on hand. Frittatas (like tacos, pizza, or fritters) are a blank canvas, basically made for improvising and using leftovers (like that lonely container of pasta in the back of the fridge or the cup or so of cauliflower you roasted for the last recipe). Use a well-seasoned cast iron skillet for this frittata; if you don't have one, butter a 9x11 inch baking dish instead.

12 eggs

½ teaspoon salt

¼ teaspoon freshly ground black pepper

2 tablespoons olive oil

½ medium onion, thinly sliced

4 cups loosely packed baby spinach

½ cup basil leaves, torn into 1-inch pieces

2 to 3 tablespoons chopped dill

½ cup whole milk or heavy cream

1 cup ricotta

1 **Heat the oven to 350°F.** In a large bowl, whisk the eggs with the salt and pepper and set aside.

2 **Cook the vegetables.** Heat the olive oil in a 12-inch skillet over medium heat. When it shimmers, add the onions and a pinch of salt and cook, stirring, until the onions soften and start to collapse, about 8 minutes. Increase the heat to medium-high and cook, stirring, until the onions just begin to brown, 2 to 3 minutes. Lower the heat to medium and add the spinach and another pinch of salt. Cook, stirring, until the spinach has cooked down and its liquid has evaporated, 3 to 4 minutes. Turn off the heat and stir in the basil and dill.

3 **Assemble the frittata.** Whisk the cream into the egg mixture and pour it over the spinach and herbs. (Or transfer the spinach and herbs to a buttered baking dish, then pour over the egg mixture.) Scatter dollops of ricotta over the top of the frittata.

4 **Bake.** Transfer to the oven and bake for 20 to 30 minutes (it will take longer if you're using a baking dish), until the frittata is puffed, pale golden brown, and just set in the center. Broil for 2 to 3 minutes to brown the top (optional). Cool for a few minutes before serving.

One and Done

THIS IS A FAMILY-FRIENDLY DISH with boatloads of flavor. I usually avoid long noodles since my boys can't resist wearing them on their heads. Fideos are thin and short, making them more manageable and less wig-like. (You can also substitute capellini broken into one-inch pieces.) A simple one-pot meal that's eaten without complaint? Yes, please.

CHICKPEAS

MAKE AHEAD!

5 MINUTES ACTIVE, 60 MINUTES TOTAL

1½ cups dry chickpeas, soaked overnight and drained

1 garlic clove, peeled

1 to 2 bay leaves

Salt, to taste

Place chickpeas in a large saucepan and cover with water by about an inch. Add the garlic clove, bay leaves, and salt. Turn the heat to medium-high and bring to a simmer. Skim and discard any foam that rises to the surface. Reduce heat and simmer for 45 to 60 minutes, until the chickpeas are tender. Taste and adjust seasoning as needed.

Fideos with Sausage and Chickpeas

35 TO 40 MINUTES · *serves 4 to 6*

4 tablespoons olive oil, divided

12 ounces chorizo, cut into ½-inch slices and quartered

1 medium onion, chopped

1 medium fennel bulb, cored and sliced

2 medium garlic cloves, peeled and chopped

1 tablespoon tomato paste

8 ounces fideo noodles

1 cup diced tomatoes

3 to 4 cups chicken stock or water

½ teaspoon salt, plus more to taste

1½ cups **COOKED CHICKPEAS** (or canned)

½ teaspoon smoked paprika

4 packed cups spinach

1 teaspoon sherry or red wine vinegar

2 tablespoons chopped parsley

Freshly ground black pepper, to taste

1 **Cook the chorizo and aromatics.** Heat a tablespoon of olive oil in a heavy-bottomed pot with a lid over medium heat. When it shimmers, add the chorizo and cook until lightly browned, then transfer to a paper towel-lined plate. Add onions, fennel, garlic, and tomato paste to the pot and cook until translucent, about 5 minutes. Transfer to a small bowl.

2 **Toast the noodles.** Add the remaining olive oil to the pan over medium-high heat. When the oil shimmers, add the fideos and cook, using tongs to turn the noodles, until they start to turn golden in spots, about 4 minutes.

3 **Add the tomatoes, stock, and salt.** Stir to combine and bring to a simmer. Cover and cook, stirring occasionally, until the noodles are cooked through, 10 to 15 minutes.

4 **Finish and serve.** Stir in the chorizo, vegetables, chickpeas, and smoked paprika. Simmer for about 5 minutes, then add the spinach and cook until it's wilted, 2 to 3 minutes. Stir in the vinegar. Taste and adjust seasoning, ladle into bowls, and garnish with a sprinkle of parsley and black pepper.

CHOOSING CHEESE

FROM 2015 TO LATE 2017, I was the food editor at *Culture*, a magazine dedicated to the wide world of cheese and the people and places behind it. There, I focused on recipes, so I was always dreaming up new dishes that incorporated my favorite cheese. I love cooking with cheese, but I really like it best on its own, on a plate with a few accompaniments.

When I worked at the magazine, I had the privilege of tasting more cheese than I knew existed in the world. I brought a lot of it home, too—much to Galen's delight and my children's suspicion. There was a point, after an event one fall, where so many leftover hunks of cheese came home to roost in our refrigerator that we had it on the table with dinner every night for a month.

We don't always have that much cheese at our disposal, but having cheese at the table shifted our dinners a little. Since it's so filling and flavorful, I don't feel like we need too many other rich things with the meal—maybe some soup; a salad or a couple of cooked vegetable dishes; pickles; some bread and sausage—a bunch of things that people can choose from and use to make their own plates (this is a smart strategy for successful dinners, cheese or not).

And like any new foods, the more they're exposed to different types of cheese, the more open the boys are to trying them. We had a French family living upstairs from us for a while, and their girls would eat any cheese set in front of them—strong blues, stinky washed rinds, you name it. So, I hold out hope. If you're new to this delightful world of milk and mold, here are a few good things to know:

- **Cheese is predominantly made from three different types of milk: cow's, sheep's, and goat's milk.** Each has a unique flavor profile, which changes depending on the style of cheese and its age.

- **Keep track of your likes and dislikes.** Write down what you've tried and what it tasted like.

- **Soft-ripened cheeses are often good gateway cheeses for children.** Try serving some brie, robiola, or a domestic variety that catches your eye. Trim the rind for the kiddos at first, but over time, encourage them to try it.

- **Don't be afraid of raw milk cheese.** Most pathogens that lead to foodborne illness in cheese develop post-production, so whether the milk is raw or pasteurized is not the issue.

- **Warm it up.** Bring cheese to room temperature before serving for optimal texture and flavor.

- **Cheese likes company.** Experiment by pairing your favorite cheeses with different fruits (fresh or dry), jams, honeys, nuts, and pickles.

Late April

SKILLET PORK CHOPS WITH RHUBARB COMPOTE •
ROASTED RADISHES

LEEK AND CHARD FRITTERS

WHITE BEANS WITH HERB PESTO •
ARUGULA SALAD • RHUBARB-RICOTTA TOAST

NEARLY NIÇOISE SALAD

SHEET PAN CHICKEN WITH POTATOES,
ARTICHOKES, AND FENNEL

SOMETIMES (LIKE IN APRIL) I forget that the ground in New England is still pretty cold in the spring and there's little local produce to come by. We bide our time with rhubarb from Oregon, artichokes from a can, and greenhouse lettuces from Vermont. We can make good until the local stuff starts growing here in earnest.

OVER THE YEARS I'VE LEARNED that there are so many little things I can do to elevate otherwise simple meals: homemade salsa spooned over a plain bowl of rice and beans; a simple and bright herby pesto; a seasonal fruit compote dolloped over whatever I choose to dollop it over. Nothing too time consuming or complex, but when I make the effort to pull together dishes like these, I get a little thrill when they take an ordinary meal into new territory. Is that too much to ask of compote?

This menu requires about two hours to get the main components out of the way. Start simple: salt the pork chops and soak the white beans the night before you prep for the week. While you're brewing your coffee the next day, get the beans on the stove and hard-boil some eggs. The rhubarb compote takes under a half hour to make. As always, if you have time, do some vegetable prep for later in the week. (Knocking out the vinaigrette and pesto now will only make your life easier midweek.)

THE BIG COOK

SOAK AND COOK THE WHITE BEANS

HARD-BOIL THE EGGS

MAKE THE RHUBARB COMPOTE

OTHER WAYS TO GET AHEAD

MAKE THE VINAIGRETTE

MAKE THE PESTO

SEASON THE CHICKEN IN ADVANCE

Good Bones

IS IT ME OR DO PORK CHOPS GET A BAD RAP? Not if you play it right. Here's how we do chops: First, when we splurge on a prime cut like this, we pay more for hormone-free, pastured pork (the kind that's also marbled with fat). Second, I buy bone-in chops. Meat on the bone always has more flavor than boneless, and bones help protect the meat from overcooking. Third, I cook them on really high heat. Your skillet is going to smoke; that's okay.

So about the splurge: Our budget means that buying high-quality meats, especially prime cuts like a loin chop, is not a weekly thing (or a monthly thing, for that matter). When we do spring for something like these chops, I keep the portions small. They are so rich and flavorful that a little goes a long way.

Roasting radishes might be new to you, but it's a must-try. When roasted, radishes lose their bite, becoming milder, almost sweet. Topped with a sprinkle of salt, some grinds of pepper, and a little chopped dill, this easy vegetable side dish is revelatory. (Not to mention so beautiful on the plate!)

RHUBARB COMPOTE

MAKE AHEAD!

5 MINUTES ACTIVE, 25 MINUTES TOTAL · *makes about 2 cups*

6 to 7 medium rhubarb stalks, cut into 2-inch pieces

1 scant cup sugar (or a little less depending on how sweet you like it)

2 tablespoons lemon juice

1-inch piece ginger, sliced into coins

3 to 4 whole star anise

Pinch of salt

Set the oven to 275°F. Toss all ingredients together in a medium baking dish and bake until the rhubarb has softened and the juices in the dish are bubbling, about 20 minutes. Remove from oven, cool, discard the ginger and anise, and refrigerate until ready to use.

Skillet Pork Chops with Rhubarb Compote · Roasted Radishes

45 MINUTES TOTAL, INCLUDING TIME TO LET PORK COME TO ROOM TEMPERATURE · *serves 4*

SKILLET PORK CHOPS

2 half-pound, center-cut, bone-in pork chops

1 teaspoon salt

¼ teaspoon freshly ground black pepper

1 tablespoon vegetable oil

4 to 5 sprigs thyme

1 cup **RHUBARB COMPOTE**

ROASTED RADISHES

1 pound red radishes, rinsed and cut in half lengthwise if large

1 tablespoon olive oil

½ teaspoon salt

Freshly ground black pepper, to taste

2 tablespoons chopped dill

1 **Prep the pork chops.** About 30 minutes before cooking, take meat out of the refrigerator and rub it with the salt and pepper.

2 **Roast the radishes.** While the pork chops are coming to room temperature, heat the oven to 425°F. Toss the radishes with olive oil and salt in a large bowl, then transfer to a rimmed baking sheet and roast until slightly wrinkled, dark around the edges, and tender, about 15 minutes. Remove from the oven and set aside.

3 **Sear the pork chops.** Turn on your hood and preheat a 12-inch skillet over high heat for about 5 minutes. It should be practically smoking. Pat the chops dry with a paper towel. Add the vegetable oil, swirl it around the pan, and add the pork chops and the thyme. Sear on one side for 2 to 3 minutes, flip, and sear again. Reduce heat to medium and continue cooking, turning and basting the pork chops in the fat they're releasing, for 4 to 5 more minutes.

4 **Check the temp.** Press a meat thermometer into the center of the chop. When it hits 145°F (medium rare), transfer the chops to a cutting board, cover loosely with foil, and let rest for about 10 minutes. The temperature of the meat will keep rising as the pork rests. After 10 minutes, it should register 150°F to 155°F (medium). Discard the thyme and carve the pork. Cut it away from the bones (discard the bones), then thinly slice.

5 **Serve.** Toss the radishes with the dill. Arrange slices of pork on plates and top with a spoonful of compote with the radishes on the side.

Leek and Chard Fritters

45 MINUTES · *serves 4*

THE ARGUMENT FOR FRITTERS (if you need one) goes something like this: Frying vegetables is a friendly way to get kids to eat them; they freeze well (make a double batch) and reheat easily, making them excellent candidates for lunch the next day; and there are few vegetables that don't taste good when they're hashed up with some aromatics and bathed in hot oil. Once you get the hang of the template, you can play around with whatever produce you have on hand, from leeks and chard to carrots and beets. These fritters are great alongside a springy salad like the Bibb Salad (pg. 274).

4 tablespoons olive oil, divided

1 leek, light green and white parts only, halved vertically and thinly sliced

1 bunch swiss chard, stems and leaves separated and chopped

½ teaspoon salt, plus more to taste

¼ cup all-purpose flour

½ teaspoon baking soda

½ cup ricotta

1 egg

2 to 3 tablespoons chopped herbs like parsley, dill, or chives

Freshly ground black pepper, to taste

Up to ¼ cup breadcrumbs

1 **Cook the vegetables.** Heat the oven to 200°F and have a baking sheet ready. Add 2 tablespoons olive oil to a large skillet over medium heat. When it shimmers, add the leeks and cook, stirring, for 2 to 3 minutes, Add the chard stems and a pinch of salt and continue to cook, stirring, until the mixture is soft and starts to cook down, another 5 to 7 minutes. Add the chopped chard leaves, stir to combine, and continue cooking until the chard is completely wilted, another 4 to 5 minutes. Remove from heat and set aside.

2 **Make the batter.** In a large bowl, whisk together the flour, baking soda, and ½ teaspoon salt. In a medium bowl, mix together the ricotta, egg, chopped herbs, and a pinch of salt and pepper. Add the cooked leeks and greens and stir to combine. Add the ricotta mixture to the dry ingredients and fold gently together to combine. If the mixture seems wet, sprinkle in some breadcrumbs, but don't go overboard or the texture will be too bready. Form into patties about 3 inches in diameter; place on a plate and refrigerate for 15 to 20 minutes. (This is a good time to make the salad!)

3 **Fritter time.** Wipe out the skillet, place it over medium heat, and add 2 tablespoons olive oil. When the oil shimmers, add the fritters. They need space to cook without steaming, so fry in small batches. Cook on each side for about 3 minutes, transfer to the baking sheet, and keep warm in the oven until ready to serve. Repeat with remaining patties.

Life's a Picnic

THIS IS ONE OF MY FAVORITE KINDS OF MEATLESS MEALS—a few simple dishes with plenty of contrasting flavors and textures. It truly is a picnic at your dinner table, where everyone can pick what they want. Worried about not feeling full on a meal like this? Don't be; there's plenty here to make a satisfying supper. If you're still unsure, just make some extra toast to dip into the beans or add a hunk of cured salami to the mix. Make this quick pesto ahead and keep it around to jazz up pretty much anything you're eating this week: hard-boiled eggs, grilled meat, roasted or raw vegetables—you name it.

A POT OF WHITE BEANS

MAKE AHEAD!

10 MINUTES ACTIVE, 2 HOURS TOTAL · *makes 6 to 7 cups*

COOKING A POT OF BEANS FROM DRIED might seem like work, but it's mostly an act of remembering (to soak, to stir) and marking time. Beans are forgiving (forgiving food is the best food)—if you don't have thyme or bay leaves, leave them out. Add parsley instead, or not. Even adding just a couple of garlic cloves will bring the beans to life nicely.

Half of these guys will be served for dinner with a swirl of pesto and a couple of side dishes; another cup will go into the Nearly Niçoise Salad. You can easily substitute canned beans, but once you get in the swing of soaking and cooking dried beans, you might find yourself doing it on the regular.

1 pound dry cannellini beans, soaked overnight

8 cups water

3 to 4 garlic cloves, peeled

2 sprigs thyme

1 to 2 bay leaves

1 dried chile (optional)

1 cup trimmings, if you have them, from leeks, celery, fennel, and parsley

1 teaspoon salt

1 **Get ready.** Rinse the beans in a colander and pick out any shriveled beans or pebbles. Transfer to a heavy-bottomed pot (I use my dutch oven) and cover with water by about an inch. Add the garlic, thyme, bay leaves, chile, and any trimmings you might have on hand.

2 **Cook.** Bring the beans to a simmer over medium-high heat. Reduce heat to medium-low and simmer for about 75 minutes. Stir in the salt, then continue simmering for another 20 to 30 minutes. The beans will take between 1½ to 2 hours to cook. (The older they are, the longer they'll take.) Add more water to keep the beans covered as needed. When tender, remove beans from heat, discard aromatics, and cool in their cooking liquid.

HERB PESTO

10 MINUTES · *makes about 1 cup*

1 medium garlic clove, peeled and roughly chopped

½ teaspoon salt

Finely grated zest of one lemon

1 cup parsley, minced

1 cup cilantro, minced

½ cup olive oil

2 tablespoons lemon juice

With a mortar and pestle or with the side of a knife on a cutting board, smash together the garlic and salt to form a paste. Place in a small bowl with the lemon zest and the herbs, then stir to combine. Drizzle in the olive oil, taste, and adjust the salt as needed. Stir in the lemon juice.

White Beans with Herb Pesto · Arugula Salad · Rhubarb-Ricotta Toast

20 MINUTES · *serves 4*

3 cups **COOKED WHITE BEANS**

HERB PESTO

RICOTTA-RHUBARB TOAST

4 to 6 slices of your favorite rustic loaf

1 tablespoon olive oil

Salt, to taste

½ cup whole milk ricotta

Freshly ground black pepper, to taste

Juice from a lemon wedge

¾ cup **RHUBARB COMPOTE**

ARUGULA SALAD

4 cups arugula

¼ cup toasted walnuts, chopped

¼ cup shaved parmesan cheese

2 to 3 tablespoons **LEMON-CHIVE VINAIGRETTE** (pg. 276)

Salt, to taste

Freshly ground black pepper, to taste

1 **Make the toast.** Heat the oven to 350°F. In a large bowl, toss the slices of bread with the olive oil and a sprinkle of salt. Place on a rimmed baking sheet and toast until crisp and browned at the edges, 5 to 8 minutes. Season the ricotta with salt and pepper; add a squeeze of lemon juice. Place both the ricotta mixture and the Rhubarb Compote in small serving bowls and place on a platter with the toasts.

2 **Heat up the beans.** While toasting the bread, put a pot of the cooked white beans on low heat to gently warm them.

3 **Make the salad.** Toss the arugula, walnuts, and parmesan in a salad bowl with the Lemon-Chive Vinaigrette. Finish with a sprinkle of salt and a few grinds of black pepper.

4 **Finish and serve.** Ladle the warmed white beans into bowls with a generous drizzle of pesto over top. Bring the salad and the platter of toasts and toppings to the table and let the gang assemble their own toasts.

Nearly Niçoise Salad

30 MINUTES · *serves 4*

I LOVE TUNA SALAD AS MUCH AS THE NEXT GAL—preferably sandwiched on white bread with Lay's potato chips shoved in there. But when I'm feeling fancy, I like to take tuna in another direction, like this simple weeknight dinner reminiscent of a classic Niçoise salad. I serve this meal on a big platter, sometimes with the components separated so the boys don't freak out. Need a hard-boiled egg refresher course? See pg. 280.

This meal, by the way, is equally ideal for a girls' weekend lunch (preferably with a bottle of cold rosé). Last note: the tuna packed in oil in a glass jar will make you rethink tuna. Give it a try!

POTATOES

1 pound new potatoes, quartered lengthwise

Salt, to taste

1 to 2 tablespoons unsalted butter

2 tablespoons chopped dill

Freshly ground black pepper, to taste

WHITE BEAN AND TUNA SALAD

4 cups arugula

2 tablespoons olive oil, divided

1 cup **COOKED WHITE BEANS**, rinsed and drained

6 ounces olive-oil-packed tuna, broken into chunks

¼ cup chopped **PICKLED RED ONIONS** (pg. 270)

1 teaspoon finely grated lemon zest

2 tablespoons chopped dill

1 teaspoon chopped parsley

Small handful Niçoise olives, pitted and torn in half

1 tablespoon lemon juice

Flaky sea salt, for sprinkling

Freshly ground black pepper, to taste

8 HARD-BOILED EGGS, sliced in half

1 **Make the potatoes.** Place the potatoes in a medium saucepan and cover with water. Add enough salt so that the water tastes briny, like seawater. Bring to a simmer over medium heat and cook until the potatoes are tender, about 10 to 15 minutes. Drain, then return to the pot and toss with the butter. Cover until ready to serve.

2 **Make the salad.** Place the arugula on a platter and drizzle with half of the olive oil. Scatter the beans over the greens, followed by the tuna, pickled red onions (if using), lemon zest, herbs, and olives. Drizzle the remaining oil over the top of the salad and add the lemon juice. Finish with a little bit of flaky sea salt and a lot of pepper.

3 **Finish and serve.** Toss the cooked potatoes with the dill and pepper; transfer to the platter alongside the salad. Add the sliced eggs to the platter and sprinkle with salt and chopped dill, if desired.

Sheet Pan Chicken with Potatoes, Artichokes, and Fennel

15 MINUTES ACTIVE, 1 HOUR TOTAL · *serves 4*

ALONGSIDE MY KNIVES AND CAST IRON SKILLETS, sheet pans are among the most important pieces of equipment in my kitchen. These dependable utility players fill a million roles in the kitchen, from baking cookies to organizing mise en place for outdoor cooking. And, of course, you can cook an entire meal on one. Easy to prep, assemble, cook, and clean up, when it's well executed, the sheet pan dinner is a wonderful thing.

I like this recipe—inspired by the *New York Times'* Melissa Clark and her sheet pan expertise—because it avoids a few of the pitfalls I've encountered when playing around with different dinners cooked this way. Adding the vegetables in stages ensures nothing turns to mush. Lemon slices in the mix keep things tasting bright. High heat gets everything crispy. One and done.

4 bone-in, skin-on chicken thighs

1 teaspoon salt, plus more to taste

1 teaspoon whole fennel seeds

1 teaspoon sweet paprika

½ teaspoon freshly ground black pepper, plus more to taste

1 pound yukon gold potatoes, cut into 1-inch chunks

½ lemon, cut into ¼-inch slices and seeded

5 to 6 sprigs thyme

2 tablespoons olive oil, divided

14-ounce can artichoke hearts, drained

½ medium leek, rinsed, dark green tops trimmed, thinly sliced

½ fennel bulb, cored and cut into ¼-inch slices

2 tablespoons chopped parsley

1 **Season the chicken.** The night before (or at least 30 minutes before cooking), put the chicken in a resealable bag with the salt, fennel, paprika, and pepper. Seal, toss to combine, and refrigerate until 30 minutes before you're ready to cook.

2 **Roast the potatoes and the chicken.** Heat the oven to 425°F. In a medium bowl, toss the potatoes, lemon slices, and thyme sprigs with a tablespoon of olive oil and a pinch of salt. Spread the potatoes on a rimmed sheet pan. Add the seasoned chicken (skin side-up), making sure that everything is in one layer to ensure even cooking and place in oven.

3 **Prepare the artichokes, leeks, and fennel.** While the chicken is roasting, quarter the artichoke hearts and pat dry with a paper towel (they should be very dry). Pat dry the leeks and fennel and toss all the vegetables together in a medium bowl with the remaining olive oil and a pinch of salt and pepper. After the chicken has been in the oven for about 15 minutes, turn the potatoes and nestle the artichoke mixture around the chicken. Roast until the chicken reaches 160°F and the leeks have crisped, about 25 minutes more. Remove from oven, sprinkle with parsley, and serve.

FIRST PICNIC OF THE SEASON!

AS SOON AS IT'S WARM AND DRY ENOUGH to sit on the ground—even if we're bundled up—we pack some food, drinks, and a blanket and head to a nearby park to break in the season. This can be March or April depending on how bad winter's been. When it's a little chilly in spring or fall, it's fun to pack a thermos of something warm that everyone can drink, like mulled cider, hot cocoa, or herbal tea with honey.

I try not to get too fancy with picnics, but I do like to bring a nice board and a couple of plastic bowls for serving because I don't like eating a meal surrounded by food packaging. It might seem a little fussy, but it makes things feel special (without a lot of extra work).

MY PICNIC TOOL KIT

Picnic blanket

Bamboo cutting board

Sharp knife with a blade guard

2 to 3 plastic or melamine bowls for serving

Cloth napkins

Melamine plates or sturdy paper plates

Utensils

IDEAS AND INSPIRATION

When I plan a picnic spread, I try to find the sweet spot between laissez-faire and over the top. I see a picnic as an excuse to make a frittata (a.k.a. use up weird odds and ends in the fridge) and cookies, shower love on some vegetables, and visit my favorite cheese shop. Whatever you bring, make sure it packs easily, travels well, tastes good at room temperature, and can generally withstand being hauled around in a bag.

Alpine cheese, salami, pickles, and bread

Hard-boiled eggs with a little container of salt and pepper

Warm slices of frittata wrapped in foil

Hummus and pita chips

Cold grilled or fried chicken legs

Crudité, a.k.a. cold vegetables and dip—radishes, sliced cucumbers and peppers, carrot sticks, blanched broccoli or cauliflower, potato wedges—with something good to dip them in. This could be as simple as some herbed yogurt or ricotta cheese whipped with a little olive oil and salt.

Nuts and fruit

Sturdy cookies or bars

May

WHOLE ROASTED FISH • HONEY-GLAZED BEETS • SPRINGTIME SNAP PEAS

SMOKED SALMON TARTINE • DEVILED EGGS • ROASTED ASPARAGUS

PASTA WITH PEA PESTO • BEET SALAD

GRILLED FLANK STEAK • ASPARAGUS-CUCUMBER SALAD IN LETTUCE CUPS

CLAIRE'S YOGURT CHICKEN

IT'S MAY, WHICH MEANS it's time to gorge on asparagus—as much as possible for as long as possible. At this time of year, those succulent stalks could slide into each and every one of my dinners and I'd be happy about it… and then I'd eat more for breakfast and lunch. It's such a short-lived treat that I can't help but overdo it. When the season ends in mid-June, I bid them a sad but satisfied goodbye.

SPRING IS FINALLY IN THE AIR so I go for fresh, light flavors and plenty of color wherever I can while cutting down on kitchen time a little. Roast some beets, make the pea pesto, cook some eggs for deviled eggs (and more for snacks), and that's it. Also, track down a whole fish (you can do it!) the day before you want to roast it. It's one item you don't want hanging around your fridge for too long. We're lucky to have an excellent source for local seafood at our Saturday farmers' market, so I'll buy it then, keep it on ice in the refrigerator, and cook it Sunday evening.

As for cooking whole fish, it's super-simple: you just season it and put it in a hot oven. Have your fishmonger scale and gut the fish for you. If you've roasted the beets ahead of time, all you need to do is heat and season them. Add some steamed jasmine or basmati rice and you're set.

THE BIG COOK

ROAST THE BEETS (PG. 272)

MAKE THE PEA PESTO

HARD-BOIL THE EGGS

PICKLE THE RED ONIONS (PG. 270)

OTHER WAYS TO GET AHEAD

MAKE THE GRAIN MUSTARD
VINAIGRETTE (PG. 276)

MARINATE THE FLANK STEAK

Feed a Boy a Fish

GROWING UP IN A COASTAL TOWN with the whiff of the fish pier always nearby (and having a dad who inhaled all shellfish in his path with impressive zeal) cemented my fish habit early on, first as an eater and later as a cook. My son, Quincy, inherited some of that gusto, but when it comes to whole fish, the main draw in our household is the heads—a true source of fascination. It's not too long before fascination turns into acceptance and both children decide it's a good idea to dig into fish, whole or otherwise. Right? It runs in the family, after all.

Whole Roasted Fish • Honey-Glazed Beets • Springtime Snap Peas

45 MINUTES ACTIVE, 1 HOUR TOTAL • *serves 4*

WHOLE ROASTED FISH

4 whole small fish, such as black sea bass (about 1 to 1½ pounds each), scaled and gutted

2 tablespoons olive oil, divided

2 teaspoons salt

1 bunch parsley, tough stems trimmed

1 lemon, zest removed and reserved

1 garlic clove, peeled and roughly chopped

1 tablespoon coriander seeds

SPRINGTIME SNAP PEAS

1 pound snap peas, ends trimmed

1 tablespoon unsalted butter

1 teaspoon lemon juice

1 to 2 tablespoons torn mint leaves

Salt, to taste

Freshly ground black pepper, to taste

HONEY-GLAZED BEETS

1 tablespoon unsalted butter

4 roasted beets, peeled and cut into wedges or coins (pg. 272)

1 teaspoon honey

1 teaspoon apple cider vinegar

1 teaspoon minced chives

½ teaspoon salt

Freshly ground black pepper, to taste

1 **Prepare the fish.** Heat the oven to 450°F and line a rimmed baking sheet with parchment paper. Pat the fish dry with a paper towel, and cut each fish with 3 diagonal slits on both sides. Rub the 4 fish all over with 1 tablespoon of the oil. Sprinkle salt over the fish and inside the cavity. Cut ½ lemon into 4 slices and place 1 slice into each fish cavity. Divide the parsley into 2 buches and set 1 bunch aside. Divide remaining parsley among each fish cavity. Roast until a meat thermometer registers 140°F, about 20 to 25 minutes.

2 **Make parsley pesto.** Roughly chop the rest of the parsley. Place chopped parsley in a food processor with remaining olive oil, lemon zest, 1 tablespoon lemon juice (from half of the lemon), coriander seeds, and a pinch of salt. Taste and adjust as needed. Set pesto aside.

3 **Blanch the snap peas.** Bring a medium pot of salted water to a boil. Add the peas and blanch until bright green, 2 to 3 minutes. Drain in a colander and rinse with cold water. Cover with some ice to stop the cooking. Set aside.

4 **Dress the beets.** While the fish is roasting, melt the butter in a medium skillet over medium heat. When it foams, add the roasted beets and toss to coat in the butter. Mix the honey and vinegar together in a small bowl and add to the pan, tossing to combine. Increase heat to medium-high and cook, stirring, until the liquid has reduced and the beets are coated in the mixture. Toss with chives, then season with salt and pepper to taste.

5 **Remove the fish from the oven.** Let it rest for 3 to 5 minutes, then transfer to a cutting board and remove the tail and fins along with the lemon slices and parsley. The filet meat should lift easily off of the bones—I use two spoons to slide the meat off and onto a plate.

6 **Finish the snap peas.** When the fish comes out of the oven, melt the butter in the pot you used to blanch the peas over medium heat. When it foams, add the blanched peas and toss to coat in the butter. Add lemon juice and toss with the mint. Sprinkle with salt and pepper to taste.

7 **Serve.** Bring the beets, peas, and fish to the table and serve with the parsley pesto.

Devil's in the Details

IS TWO POUNDS OF ASPARAGUS TOO MUCH? Not for me. It always gets eaten, if not at dinner then during cleanup or breakfast. For these tartines, I forgo the predictable schmear of cream cheese and instead beat goat cheese with yogurt and a little lemon to amp up the tartness. This makes the spread a light, bright foil to the salmon. Delicious, quick, easy. Did I mention this is my ideal meal?

Smoked Salmon Tartine · Deviled Eggs · Roasted Asparagus

30 MINUTES · *serves 4*

DEVILED EGGS

8 LARGE HARD-BOILED EGGS (see pg. 280 for tips)

¼ cup mayonnaise

1 tablespoon grated horseradish

½ teaspoon salt

¼ cup **PICKLED RED ONIONS**, chopped (pg. 270)

Freshly ground black pepper, to taste

2 tablespoons chopped chives

SMOKED SALMON TARTINE

8 slices of your favorite country bread

1 to 2 tablespoons olive oil

Salt, to taste

4 ounces goat cheese

1 ounce whole milk yogurt

1 teaspoon lemon juice, plus more to taste

1 teaspoon finely grated lemon zest

Flaky sea salt, to taste

Freshly ground black pepper, to taste

4 ounces smoked salmon

2 tablespoons chopped dill

ROASTED ASPARAGUS

2 pounds asparagus, ends snapped off

2 tablespoons olive oil

Flaky sea salt

Lemon juice, to taste

Freshly ground black pepper, to taste

1 **Devil the eggs.** Peel the eggs under running water, then halve each lengthwise. Scoop the yolks into a medium bowl. Use the tines of a fork to break up the yolks. Add the mayonnaise and continue stirring and smooshing the mixture (technical term). Add the horseradish and salt. Stir in the pickled red onions (if using) and some pepper to taste. Use a small spoon to return the egg yolk mixture to the whites. Sprinkle with chives.

2 **Time to toast.** Heat the oven to 350°F. Toss the bread with the olive oil and salt and arrange on a rimmed baking sheet. Bake until the bread is crisp, golden, and slightly dark around the edges, 5 to 8 minutes. Remove from oven.

3 **Prepare the tartine.** While the bread is toasting, mix the goat cheese and yogurt together in a small bowl with the lemon juice and zest. Stir in salt and pepper to taste. Spread mixture onto the toasts, then top each with a slice of smoked salmon. Garnish with chopped dill, a tiny pinch of salt, and a bit of pepper.

4 **Roast the asparagus.** When the bread comes out of the oven, increase the heat to 425°F. Spread it out in a single layer onto 1 or 2 rimmed baking sheets. Sprinkle with olive oil and salt. Roast for 12 to 15 minutes (a little longer if you like it crispy at the tips), until the asparagus is bright green and starts to darken. Transfer to a large platter and squeeze some lemon juice over the top, followed by a sprinkle of salt and pepper and serve.

Keeping it Simple

THIS PESTO is a fast, delicious crowd pleaser based on one freezer staple (peas) and one fridge staple (ricotta). Here, I toss it with pasta, but I also love to spread it over toasts for a quick dinner or an elegant party-ready appetizer. The light texture and fresh flavors make this an easy spring dish no matter how you serve it.

PEA PESTO

10 MINUTES · *makes about 2 cups*

10 ounces peas (thawed if frozen)

1 cup ricotta

½ teaspoon salt

1 to 2 tablespoons lemon juice

1 to 2 tablespoons olive oil

1 to 2 teaspoons freshly grated lemon zest

Combine the peas, ricotta, salt, and lemon juice in a blender and buzz until smooth. Slowly drizzle in the olive oil. Transfer to a storage container and stir in the lemon zest. Taste and adjust seasoning. Cover and refrigerate until ready to use.

Pasta with Pea Pesto · Beet Salad

10 MINUTES ACTIVE, 20 MINUTES TOTAL · *serves 4*

PASTA WITH PEA PESTO

1 pound penne

1 to 2 tablespoons olive oil

1½ cups **PEA PESTO**

¼ cup torn mint leaves, divided

2 tablespoons minced chives

2 tablespoons shaved parmesan

Freshly ground black pepper, to taste

BEET SALAD

2 cups arugula

½ medium fennel bulb, cored and thinly sliced

Salt, to taste

Freshly ground black pepper, to taste

2 to 3 **ROASTED BEETS**, peeled and diced (see pg. 272 for tips)

¼ cup shelled pistachios or toasted walnuts, finely chopped

GRAIN MUSTARD VINAIGRETTE (pg. 276)

1 **Prepare the pasta.** Cook the pasta according to package directions in a large pot of salted water. Drain (reserve ¼ cup pasta water) and toss with a drizzle of olive oil. Add the pea pesto and half of the mint, tossing well to evenly coat the pasta. If necessary, thin the pesto with a little pasta water, then transfer to a large serving bowl. Garnish with the remaining mint and the chives, parmesan, and pepper.

2 **Assemble the salad.** Toss the arugula and fennel in a salad bowl with 2 to 3 tablespoons of the vinaigrette and a pinch of salt and pepper. Toss the beets in a small bowl with another tablespoon or so of the vinaigrette, then scatter the beets over the greens. Season with salt and pepper and add the chopped nuts.

Grilled Flank Steak · Asparagus-Cucumber Salad in Lettuce Cups

45 MINUTES · *serves 4*

I LIKE TO SERVE THIS STEAK AND SALAD with leaves of bibb lettuce and encourage my kids to make this a lettuce cup situation. This is successful most of the time, and it reminds me that sometimes all you need for a pleasant dinner scenario is some solid product presentation.

Flank steak takes well to marinades, cooks quickly, and translates easily into second-day meals. Here, I keep the flavors lively and the portions small—and let the vegetables fill us up.

GRILLED FLANK STEAK

1½ to 2 pounds flank steak

1 teaspoon salt

1 large garlic clove, peeled and chopped

Zest of 1 lime

1 fresno chile, seeded and thinly sliced

2 teaspoons coriander seeds, lightly crushed

1 tablespoon brown sugar

1 teaspoon fish sauce

1 to 2 tablespoons olive oil

ASPARAGUS-CUCUMBER SALAD

½ small red onion, thinly sliced

¼ to ½ teaspoon salt

1 teaspoon brown sugar

3 tablespoons rice wine vinegar

1 teaspoon fish sauce

1 tablespoon lime juice

1 bunch asparagus, blanched and cooled

1 cucumber, peeled and seeded

1 small red bell pepper, seeded and diced

1 tablespoon olive oil

½ cup chopped mint

¼ cup chopped cilantro

1 head bibb lettuce, leaves removed and kept whole

1 **Season the steak.** The night or morning before cooking, place the flank steak in a resealable plastic bag with the remaining ingredients and refrigerate. About 30 minutes before you're ready to cook, remove steak from the fridge.

2 **Grill the steak.** Light a charcoal or gas grill to high heat. Remove steak from marinade and lightly pat dry. When the grill is hot, place the steak over the hottest part and cook for 3 to 4 minutes. Flip and cook for another 3 minutes, then move to a cooler spot on the grill, cover, and cook for another 2 to 3 minutes. For medium-rare steak, the temperature should be about 125°F; for medium, about 135°F. Transfer the steak to a cutting board and cover with foil. Let rest for 10 minutes.

3 **Make the salad.** Meanwhile, add the onions to a small bowl with the salt, sugar, vinegar, fish sauce, and lime juice. Stir to combine and set aside. Chop the asparagus into 1-inch pieces and cut the cucumber into ¼-inch half moons. Set aside. When the steak comes off the grill to rest, add the asparagus, cucumber, and bell pepper to the bowl with the onions. Add the olive oil and chopped herbs, toss together, taste, and adjust seasoning.

4 **Finish and serve.** Thinly slice the steak and place on a platter with the Asparagus-Cucumber Salad. Serve with the lettuce leaves for those who want to make lettuce cups.

Claire's Yogurt Chicken

40 MINUTES · *serves 4*

I KNEW MY FRIEND CLAIRE AND I would get along famously when, soon after meeting her, I heard her declare butter to be a health food. This recipe is inspired by a dish she makes, but with white meat instead of dark. I find using breast meat lightens things up a bit and lets the tangy, spicy yogurt sauce take center stage. As you've surely noticed by now, I frequently toss spinach into whatever I'm cooking so I can say we ate our vegetables without having to prepare anything extra. I serve it all over basmati rice (pg. 280).

1½ pounds boneless, skinless chicken breasts

2 teaspoons salt, divided, plus more to taste

3 tablespoons vegetable oil, divided

2 medium garlic cloves, peeled and grated

1-inch piece ginger, peeled and grated

½ teaspoon ground turmeric, plus more to taste

½ teaspoon sweet paprika or Aleppo pepper

½ teaspoon ground cumin

½ teaspoon ground coriander

½ cup diced tomatoes

1½ cups plain whole milk yogurt (not Greek yogurt)

½ teaspoon mustard seeds

2 cups spinach (optional)

Juice of ½ lemon

2 to 4 tablespoons chopped cilantro

1 **Prepare the chicken.** Cut the chicken into 1-inch pieces and pat dry. Toss with 1½ teaspoons salt and set aside.

2 **Prepare the sauce.** Add 1 tablespoon of the oil to a dutch oven (or a large sauté pan with a lid) over medium heat. When the oil shimmers, add the garlic and ginger and cook, stirring, for 1 minute. Stir in the turmeric, paprika, cumin, and coriander and cook for another minute. Add a splash of water if the spices stick to the pot. Add the tomatoes and cook, stirring, for another 2 to 3 minutes. Stir in the yogurt and remaining ½ teaspoon salt and transfer to a food processor or blender. Process until smooth and thoroughly combined.

3 **Cook the chicken.** Wipe out the pan and add the remaining oil over medium-high heat. When the oil shimmers, add the chicken. Cook, stirring, turning the pieces until no longer pink on the outside, 5 to 6 minutes. During the last minute, add the mustard seeds and continue to cook, stirring, until they pop, about 1 minute. Pour the sauce over the chicken and stir to combine.

4 **Finish and serve.** Bring the mixture to a simmer, then reduce heat to medium-low and cover the pot. Cook until chicken is cooked through, another 12 to 15 minutes. Reduce heat to low, add the spinach if using, stir to combine, and simmer until fully wilted. Stir in the lemon juice. Season to taste, serve over rice, and sprinkle with cilantro.

BATCH THAT

ONE OF THE MOST OBVIOUS WAYS my cooking has changed since having children is that I batch cook whenever possible. Whether it's grains, beans, hard-boiled eggs, or roasted or blanched vegetables, your future self will thank you for getting a few ingredients prepared in advance. On evenings when we're home late, being able to peel and serve a few eggs in less than five minutes is huge. It saves us from meltdowns and gives me space to cook dinner.

Batch cooking doesn't need to be an all-day affair. You can slide a batch of beets into the oven while roasting a different vegetable for dinner. Eggs take ten minutes—cook them while you're making coffee. Or stick a pot of beans or barley on the stove one evening after the kids have gone to bed.

Once you have a few things cooked and stored, you're that much closer to pulling together quick snacks, sides, lunches, and so forth. Here are some of my favorite things to batch cook:

....

Barley, wheat berries, and other grains: Follow the package directions and then spread out on a sheet pan to cool. Toss with a little oil and salt and refrigerate until ready to use. Sprinkle over salads, turn them into a side dish, or build a grain bowl with odds and ends from the fridge. Simmer with a little milk, dried fruit, and maple syrup and see if you can convince anyone to eat it for breakfast. Like oatmeal! Cooked grains keep in the fridge for about a week; I also recently learned from cookbook author Maria Speck that you can spread them flat in a resealable bag and freeze them, which is genius.

Blanched green vegetables: Here's a small piece of work that really makes me feel like a grownup when I pull it off. Come home from the grocery store or market and boil a big pot of salty water. While you wait, trim, peel, and rinse your green vegetables—anything from broccoli and green beans to kale and collard greens—then blanch them briefly in the boiling water until they are bright green and slightly tender. Chill in a bowl of ice water, then pat dry and store in the fridge. Get in the habit and you'll save a bunch of time when dinner rolls around, make green vegetables more readily available for snacking, and extend their life in the refrigerator.

Meatballs: I often make double batches of things that take some time and effort—once you're in cooking mode you might as well, right? Stick that second batch in the freezer and you can count on an effortless meal sometime down the road. This category includes soups and stews, turnovers, and most definitely meatballs. Sometimes I go all out and make a triple batch with sauce, then bag and freeze the extra portions. During a busy week, all I need to do for dinner is pull a bag from the freezer, boil water for pasta, and toss up a quick salad. Meatballs and sauce have near-universal appeal, making them a safe bet to bring to new parents or anyone else who needs a fix of home cooking in their life.

Early June

**ROAST SALMON • SNAP PEAS •
POTATOES AND DILL**

**SOBA NOODLES WITH SALMON, SNAP PEAS,
AND BOK CHOY**

BIG SNACKS

**CORNMEAL WAFFLES WITH YOGURT AND
STRAWBERRIES**

LAMB TURNOVERS

JUNE IS STRAWBERRY SEASON, which means working those delicate beauties into every meal possible. June also means end-of-year school and sports activities and a packed calendar. These are the times that call for a solid plan (with strawberries) that gives you some flexibility.

Oh wait, June also means wild-caught Alaskan salmon. Like asparagus (but even more luxurious), salmon is one of those ingredients I wait for all spring. It's a splurge, but worth it to enjoy such a beautiful seasonal food and support the Alaskan salmon fishery (one of the most well-managed fisheries in the country) while I'm at it.

LEFTOVER FISH MAKES ME THINK OF that special person in your office who puts theirs in the microwave (why). Fish certainly isn't the first thing that comes to mind when you think about batch cooking, but there are notable exceptions, salmon being one. Because it's so rich and meaty, it doesn't lose much flavor or texture by spending a night in the fridge (unlike, say, flounder). I roast a large portion for a straightforward salmon meal one night, and I repurpose half of it for dinner the next night. Here, I toss it with cold soba noodles, but we're talking about wild salmon— it's going to taste good no matter what you do. Luxe it up: Try it in an omelet with minced fresh tarragon; flake it into an arugula salad with sliced native strawberries and crumbled chevre; or toss it into a lemon-cream pasta with wilted spinach.

If you budget ninety minutes to get the prep for this menu done, you should be in good shape. Pull the puff pastry from the freezer the night before and let it thaw overnight in the refrigerator.

THE BIG COOK

MAKE THE LAMB TURNOVERS

PREP THE SNAP PEAS AND BOK CHOY

OTHER WAYS TO GET AHEAD

PUT THE FROZEN PUFF PASTRY DOUGH IN THE REFRIGERATOR TO DEFROST

MAKE THE HERBY YOGURT SAUCE TO SERVE WITH TURNOVERS (PG. 277)

MIX THE DRY WAFFLE INGREDIENTS

COOK THE SOBA NOODLES

Simple Pleasures

BECAUSE WILD-CAUGHT SALMON is so distinct and delicious, I keep the flavors in this meal pretty straightforward. Spoon a quick yogurt-dijon sauce over the fish (it's good for dipping your potatoes into, too), squeeze a little lemon over the snap peas, toss the potatoes in butter and dill, and leave it at that.

The main thing to keep in mind is that you're roasting all of the fish on one night and then tucking half of it away for another dinner. So you'll cut a side of salmon in half, and then cut one of those halves into four filets. The other half you'll cook in one big piece, which will take slightly longer than the four smaller filets.

Roast Salmon · Snap Peas · Potatoes and Dill

35 MINUTES · *serves 4*

SNAP PEAS

1 pound snap peas, ends trimmed

1 tablespoon unsalted butter

1 teaspoon lemon juice

Salt, to taste

Freshly ground black pepper, to taste

POTATOES AND DILL

1 pound new potatoes, quartered lengthwise

1 to 2 tablespoons unsalted butter

2 tablespoons chopped dill

Salt, to taste

Freshly ground black pepper, to taste

ROAST SALMON

1½ pounds wild-caught Alaskan salmon

4 tablespoons canola oil, divided

Salt, to taste

Lemon wedges

YOGURT-DIJON SAUCE

½ cup plain whole milk yogurt

2 tablespoons dijon mustard

1 teaspoon lemon juice

Salt, to taste

Freshly ground black pepper, to taste

1 **Blanch the snap peas.** Bring a medium pot of salted water to a boil. Add the snap peas and blanch for 2 to 3 minutes, until bright green. Drain in a colander and rinse with cold water. Add a few ice cubes to the colander to stop the cooking and set aside.

2 **Make the potatoes.** Place the potatoes in a medium saucepan and cover with water. Add enough salt so that the water tastes briny, like seawater. Bring to a simmer over medium heat and cook until the potatoes are tender when poked with the tip of a paring knife, 10 to 15 minutes. Drain, then return to the pot and toss with the butter and dill, and add salt and pepper to taste.

3 **Roast the salmon.** (Remember, you'll be cooking all of the salmon for 2 separate meals.) Heat the oven to 425°F. Place a large, oven-safe skillet over high heat. Cut the salmon filet into 2 equal pieces. Add 2 tablespoons oil to the pan and when it shimmers, add a piece of salmon, skin-side down. Cook without disturbing until the salmon lightens in color around the skin, 3 to 5 minutes. Transfer to the oven and roast until the salmon is just cooked through, an additional 7 to 10 minutes. Transfer to a plate and set aside to cool. Wipe out the skillet and return it to the stovetop. When cool, store this piece of salmon in the refrigerator for dinner later this week.

Cut the other half of the salmon into 4 equal filets and lightly sprinkle both sides with salt. Add remaining 2 tablespoons oil to the pan and when it shimmers, add the salmon filets, skin-side down. Cook without disturbing until the salmon lightens in color around the skin, 3 to 5 minutes. Transfer to the oven and roast until the salmon is just cooked through, an additional 5 to 8 minutes.

4 **Make the yogurt-dijon sauce.** Stir the yogurt together with the mustard and lemon juice, add salt and pepper to taste, and set aside.

5 **Fix up your peas.** When the fish comes out of the oven, melt the butter in the pot you used to blanch the peas over medium heat. When it foams, add the peas and toss to coat. Add a squeeze of lemon juice and sprinkle with salt and pepper to taste. Warm up the potatoes if you like.

6 **Serve.** Plate the salmon filets, snap peas, and potatoes. Spoon a little yogurt-dijon sauce over the fish, sprinkle with some chopped dill, and add a lemon wedge to each plate.

Soba Noodles with Salmon, Snap Peas, and Bok Choy

25 MINUTES · *serves 4 to 6*

TO GET THE MOST OUT OF YOUR SECOND-DAY SALMON, don't fuss with it much. I usually go for a meal where I can flake in the fish straight from the fridge, and if it gets heated (in warm pasta, for example), I keep the heat gentle. Here, salmon is tossed into a cold soba noodle salad and dressed with rice wine vinegar (which highlights the fish's mildly sweet notes). This is a super flavorful meal. Listen: if you ended up eating all the salmon last night, I can't say I blame you. Just throw in some more vegetables and call it a day.

1 pound soba noodles

1 teaspoon sesame oil

1 to 2 teaspoons rice wine vinegar

1 teaspoon soy sauce, plus more to taste

1 tablespoon canola or safflower oil

1 medium garlic clove, peeled and chopped

2 medium heads bok choy, thinly sliced

½ pound snap peas, trimmed and thinly sliced on the diagonal

½ red bell pepper, diced

½ pound **SALMON**, roasted, skin removed, and flaked into bite-size pieces

1 to 2 tablespoons toasted sesame seeds

1 sheet toasted nori, cut into thin 1-inch-long pieces (optional)

1 **Cook the soba noodles.** Bring a pot of salted water to a boil and cook the noodles according to package directions. Drain in a colander and rinse with cold water to cool noodles. Shake off excess water, use a paper towel to blot if needed, then toss with sesame oil and transfer to a storage container. Refrigerate until ready to use.

2 **Dress the noodles.** Toss the cooled noodles in a large bowl with rice wine vinegar and soy sauce. Set aside.

3 **Cook the vegetables.** Add the oil to a medium skillet over medium heat. When the oil is warm, add the garlic and cook for one minute. Add the bok choy and cook, stirring, for 3 to 5 minutes, until the greens have wilted and the white parts are tender but still have some crunch. Add a drizzle of soy sauce to taste.

4 **Toss and serve.** Transfer the bok choy to the bowl with the soba noodles. Add the snap peas, red bell pepper, and salmon and toss to combine. Taste and adjust the seasoning. Serve in bowls and garnish with sesame seeds and nori.

Big Snacks

HERE'S SOMETHING YOU ALREADY KNEW: not every night is a gustatory occasion. What about when one child's end-of-year school picnic coincides with another child's baseball practice; when school pickup and a last-minute downtown meeting are at the same time; when work goes late and you sit in traffic, making you late for the next thing on the docket?

For those nights, there is takeout. There are also snack platters and meals that make it to the plate in no time. Here's what I'm talking about.

Fried Rice: Mince an onion or scallion and garlic and cook in a skillet with a splash of oil. Hash up any cooked vegetable (or shred a carrot and some cabbage) and add to the pan. Add leftover rice, turn up the heat, and cook, tossing, until heated through. Slide into a bowl, fry some eggs, lay those over the rice, sprinkle on some soy sauce, sesame seeds, and scallion greens, and get on with it.

Quesadillas: We buy cheddar cheese and tortillas in bulk so we're never without this option. Sprinkle ¼ cup shredded cheese in between two tortillas and toss in a few additions—frozen vegetables are great here. Try corn or finely chopped spinach or broccoli. Heat in a skillet until the cheese is melted and the vegetables are warm and serve with salsa.

Snack Attack: Use up leftovers and clean out your fridge. Carrot and celery sticks, a bowl of peanut butter, a bowl of hummus (see pg. 279 for my homemade versions). Hard-boiled eggs, nuts, and dried fruit. Apple slices, ham and cheese rollups, bread and butter—you get the picture.

Breakfast for Dinner: Homemade granola (see pg. 251) with yogurt and fruit; egg and cheese breakfast sandwiches on bagels or english muffins. Got pesto from earlier in the week hanging in the fridge? Smear some on that sandwich. I rarely have time to fix up a big breakfast in the morning, so moving these meals to dinnertime lets me play. (Flip the page to see one of our favorites.)

Cornmeal Waffles with Yogurt and Strawberries

35 MINUTES · *serves 4*

HOORAY, BREAKFAST FOR DINNER! These hearty, crunchy waffles, based on a recipe I've made for years from the *Joy of Cooking*, are a perfect vehicle for peak-season strawberries and a few spoonfuls of yogurt. (Looking for something more savory? I also really like these with black beans, salsa, and a fried egg on top.)

To get the waffles nice and crisp, let them cook longer than your waffle maker tells you to (I usually give them another three minutes or so). Remaining waffles can be frozen and reheated in the toaster for breakfast.

1 cup all-purpose flour

1 cup coarse ground cornmeal

2 teaspoons baking powder

½ teaspoon baking soda

¾ teaspoon salt

2 cups buttermilk

4 tablespoons unsalted butter, melted and cooled

2 tablespoons maple syrup

2 eggs, separated

TO SERVE

Whole milk yogurt

1 quart strawberries, hulled and halved

Maple syrup

1 **Mix the batter.** Heat the oven to 200°F. Preheat a waffle maker and place a cooling rack on a rimmed baking sheet. In a large bowl, combine the flour, cornmeal, baking powder and soda, and salt. In a medium bowl, whisk together the buttermilk, melted butter, maple syrup, and egg yolks. Pour the liquid ingredients into the dry ones and mix together, taking care not to overmix. Beat the egg whites with an electric mixer until they form soft peaks, then gently fold into the waffle batter.

2 **Make the waffles.** Use a liquid measuring cup to pour 4 to 6 ounces of batter onto the heated waffle maker. Close and cook until the waffle maker signals it's done—and then keep going (see headnote). When the first waffles are done, transfer to the baking sheet and place in the oven. Repeat until all waffles are cooked.

3 **Serve.** Dollop yogurt over the waffles followed by strawberries and a drizzle of maple syrup.

Freezer Gold

THESE RICH LITTLE PASTRIES don't need much more than a salad to make a complete meal. (Try the chickpea salad on pg. 279—it's the perfect match.) And they're the ultimate freezer stash. Once you're done rolling and filling and folding and crimping, set aside however many you want to cook right then, then transfer the rest to a sheet pan and freeze. Once they've hardened, transfer to a freezer bag. On some upcoming too-busy night, pull them out, bake (add a few minutes to the cooking time), make a salad, and you're good to go.

Last word: turnovers are a great template for any number of variations. You don't have to stick with lamb; you could do beef or a combination of sautéed and seasoned vegetables. Puff pastry + tasty filling + a dipping sauce = dinner joy. The options are endless. (Just remember to put that puff pastry in the fridge the day before you want to use it so you're not staring at a hunk of frozen pastry when you're ready to work.)

LAMB TURNOVERS

1 HOUR · *makes 16 turnovers*

1 tablespoon olive oil

½ medium yellow onion, finely chopped

3 garlic cloves, peeled and chopped

2 tablespoons tomato paste

½ teaspoon salt, plus more to taste

1 teaspoon ground cumin

1 teaspoon ground coriander

½ teaspoon cinnamon

½ teaspoon freshly ground black pepper

1 pound ground lamb

2 tablespoons pomegranate molasses

¼ cup packed parsley leaves, chopped

¼ cup mint leaves, chopped

1 to 2 teaspoons lemon juice

3 eggs, divided

1-pound sheet puff pastry, thawed

TO SERVE

Herby Yogurt Sauce, pg. 277

Chickpea Salad, pg. 279

1 **Make the filling.** Add the olive oil to a large skillet over medium heat. When it's warm, add the onion and garlic and cook, stirring, for 2 to 3 minutes. Stir in the tomato paste, cook for another 1 to 2 minutes, add the salt and spices, and cook until the spices are fully combined, about another minute. Add the lamb and cook, stirring, until it is fully browned, about 5 minutes. Stir in the molasses and cook for about 2 more minutes. Remove pan from heat and add the parsley, mint, and lemon juice. Add an egg and stir until combined. Taste and adjust the seasoning. Set aside.

2 **Prepare the dough.** Heat the oven to 400°F and line 2 rimmed baking sheets with parchment paper. Dust a work surface with flour and unfold the puff pastry onto it. Roll into a 16-inch square and cut into quarters. Transfer 3 of the quarters to one of the baking sheets (in 1 layer so they don't stick to each other) and refrigerate until you're ready to use.

3 **Fill and form the turnovers.** Lightly beat the second egg in a small bowl and set aside. Working 1 dough section at a time, cut each square into 4 smaller squares. Place 1 heaping tablespoon of filling onto the center of each square, then brush all of the edges of the pastry with the beaten egg. Fold 1 corner over to meet the opposite corner to form a triangle, then press down along the edges to seal. Use the tines of a fork or your fingers to crimp the edges. Transfer to the remaining rimmed baking sheet. Repeat until you have 16 turnovers.

4 **Finish.** With the third egg, make the egg wash. Arrange 8 turnovers on one of the parchment-lined baking sheets, brush with egg wash, and bake until deep golden and puffed, about 20 minutes. Assemble the remaining turnovers on the baking sheet and place in the freezer. Once they're frozen, transfer to a freezer bag until ready to serve.

5 **Serve.** Whip up a quick yogurt sauce, and serve alongside the turnovers and a salad.

GROW SOME FOOD

AS A CITY DWELLER, I fantasize about the day we'll have a yard big enough to do some serious gardening—of both the flower and vegetable varieties. Until then, I do a little bit of both. While I love flowers and perennials, growing some of your own food is extremely satisfying—not to mention fun and engaging for the kids. What I love about having a garden is that I can take what I need and leave the rest in the ground. One does not always need an entire bunch of cilantro or dill (although I always do my best to use them up regardless); sometime a sprig or two will do the trick.

I've grown basil, cilantro, and parsley; red lettuce, green leaf lettuce, and romaine; snap peas, green and yellow beans; carrots, cucumbers, kale, and broccoli rabe in my four-by-six-foot raised bed, plus a few annual flowers for cutting. I grow sage, thyme, lavender, and rosemary in my perennial beds. I also attempted a few cherry tomato plants, but I didn't give them big enough pots, so they withered. There's always next year.

Even if you don't have the space (or desire) for a raised bed, you can grow herbs in pots or modular raised beds. My neighbor has super cool planters on wheels so she can move them around depending on what she's growing and how much sun it needs.

Herbs are especially fun to grow, and many of them—like cilantro, parsley, dill, and chervil—start easily from seed. As long as you have some sun, you can grow herbs in pots on a deck, porch, or fire escape. If you get a green thumb going and want more space, see if there are community gardens around you. I used to belong to one and it was a great way to experiment and learn from more experienced gardeners. I was amazed by how much food people could grow in their little plots.

My kids helped me plant the first round of seeds in the garden this spring, and they are always excited when something tangible comes out of the ground (they loved the carrots last year). Between that excitement, the great homegrown flavor, and the usefulness of being able to pick just what you need when you need it, why not dig in?

Late June

**HONEY-MUSTARD CHICKEN •
GRILLED PEPPERS AND ZUCCHINI**

NACHOS WITH BITS AND BOBS

**PASTA SALAD WITH ZUCCHINI AND HERBS •
ROASTED SHRIMP AND TOMATO SKEWERS**

PANZANELLA

SUMMER ROLLS

IN THE WARM WEATHER, I would grill outside every night if I could. But sometimes our beloved charcoal grill is just too much trouble on a busy night. So when I do grill, I throw all sorts of food on the grates (pizza, lemons, fruit) and make sure to cook extra for dinners and lunches throughout the week. It's a win-win: cooking out is (mostly) super fun, and having extra prepped ingredients on hand—well, that's the name of the game.

THE JOY OF SUMMER FARE, for me anyway, is simplifying the cooking. I tend toward flexible dishes that can absorb the bits and pieces of whatever's popping in the garden or at the farmers' market. In these warm, languid months, when routines have either slowed way down or gone out the window altogether, I plan my week with recipes like the ones included here. I keep things light and rely on seasonal ingredients that do double duty over the course of the week.

Grilled chicken is a workhorse in the summer. One night you can serve it up with a tangy honey mustard and grilled vegetables hot off of the grill; the next night that same batch of chicken can be thrown into a nacho feast. Summer rolls are also a household favorite here; they're another hands-on meal that requires next to no actual cooking (hello, summer goals).

The rule I live by in the summer is to know my limits, and a hot kitchen is one of them. I tend to swap my long-simmered dried beans for the canned variety for this reason. And so I don't have a pasta pot and a hot oven going at the same time on some steamy evening, I find a morning to cook pasta for the pasta salad. I'll scoop out the pasta, leave the water in the pot, and blanch the rice noodles, followed by the shrimp (for summer rolls), too. This keeps the boiling to a minimum and extends the shrimp's freshness.

Some do-ahead work this week includes seasoning the chicken at least thirty minutes or the night before you grill it. Thread the shrimp skewers up to two days in advance of when you plan on cooking and eating them. Nothing major, but it's good to get steps out of the way when you can.

THE BIG COOK

SEASON AND GRILL THE CHICKEN

PREP AND GRILL THE PEPPERS AND ZUCCHINI

MAKE THE SMOKY REFRIED PINTOS

OTHER WAYS TO GET AHEAD

COOK THE PASTA FOR THE PASTA SALAD

BLANCH THE SHRIMP AND COOK THE RICE NOODLES FOR THE SUMMER ROLLS

PICKLE THE RED ONIONS (PG. 270)

MAKE THE VINAIGRETTE FOR THE PASTA SALAD

Honey-Mustard Chicken · Grilled Peppers and Zucchini

1 HOUR · *serves 4*

HERE'S A STRAIGHTFORWARD AND DELICIOUS SUMMER MEAL. A couple of tips: Pat the chicken dry before grilling; otherwise it could steam a little, which prevents the skin from getting crisp. Glaze toward the end of cooking—too early and the glaze will burn. You need oil on the vegetables to help carry the smoky flavors of the grill, but use it sparingly—too much and it will cause flare-ups and scorch the peppers and zucchini. After the vegetables come off the grill, I usually drizzle on a little extra oil along with lemon juice or vinegar and chopped herbs.

The chicken and vegetables you grill today can be used for a number of meals throughout the week. I'll often remove the skin and shred the chicken when I'm cleaning up from this meal—it's easier to do at that point, as opposed to after it's been refrigerated.

HONEY-MUSTARD CHICKEN

3 to 4 pounds bone-in, skin-on chicken legs and thighs, trimmed of extra fat

2 teaspoons salt, plus more to taste

Freshly ground black pepper, to taste

2 sprigs rosemary

½ cup honey

½ cup dijon mustard

GRILLED PEPPERS AND ZUCCHINI

4 to 5 red bell peppers

2 to 3 medium green zucchini

1 to 2 teaspoons olive oil, plus more to taste

Salt, to taste

Freshly ground black pepper, to taste

½ lemon

Leaves from 1 to 2 sprigs marjoram or oregano

1 **Season the chicken.** The night before cooking, place the chicken in a large plastic bag and add about 2 teaspoons of salt, a few grinds of pepper, and the rosemary sprigs. Refrigerate overnight.

2 **Light the grill.** Remove the chicken from the refrigerator and pat dry. Discard the rosemary. Light the grill. If you're working on a gas grill, turn the heat on one side to medium-high and on the other side to low. If you have a charcoal grill, start the charcoal in a chimney. When it's ready, dump into a pile on one side of the grill and spread it out so the heat will be evenly distributed on that side. Let the coals burn down (or the gas grill heat up) and clean the grate if necessary.

3 **Make the glaze.** While the coals are burning down, whisk together the honey and mustard in a small bowl, add salt and pepper to taste, and set aside.

4 **Prep the vegetables.** Stand the peppers vertically on the cutting board and cut lengthwise into into 3 pieces, removing stems and seeds. Cut the tops and bottoms off of the zucchini and cut lengthwise into long strips about

½-inch thick. Place the vegetables in a large bowl, drizzle with 1 to 2 teaspoons of oil, sprinkle with salt, and set aside.

5 **Grill the chicken.** When the grill is ready, place the chicken, skin-side down, on the hotter grate (depending on the size of the grill, you may need to do this in batches). Sear, uncovered, for 3 to 4 minutes on each side. Move the chicken to the cooler side of the grill. Cover, making sure to leave the air intake (the little holes in the top of the cover) open. After about 5 minutes, turn the chicken pieces. If some don't have enough char, return them to the hot side for a few minutes.

6 **Glaze the chicken.** Brush the chicken pieces with the honey-mustard glaze and cover the grill. After 2 to 3 minutes, turn the chicken and brush the other side with glaze. Cover again for another 2 to 3 minutes. Uncover the grill, turn the chicken, and brush with more glaze if you like.

7 **Take the chicken's temperature.** When it reaches 160°F, remove the chicken from the grill and onto a platter and cover with foil. Portion out 1 to 2 pieces of chicken per person for the meal and reserve the rest for meals later this week.

8 **Grill the vegetables and lemon.** When you take the chicken off the grill, place the sliced vegetables, along with the ½ lemon (cut-side down), on the hotter side. Cook for 3 to 4 minutes on each side. Move to the cooler side of the grill and continue cooking for another 1 to 2 minutes if needed. Remove from grill, let cool, and store half of the peppers and zucchini in the refrigerator.

9 **Finish and serve.** Place remaining peppers and zucchini on a platter and drizzle with a little oil. Squeeze the grilled lemon over the top, sprinkle with salt and pepper, and scatter with the marjoram or oregano leaves. Serve everything family style.

Top Notch Nachos

NACHOS ARE A PERFECTLY VIABLE DINNER OPTION. They're a crowd pleaser, a great vehicle for using up bits and bobs, and they don't require utensils (more summer goals). If I were to make nachos just for me (ha!), I'd layer in as many ingredients as possible to increase the odds of finding that perfect loaded chip. But my kids like theirs pretty plain, with just chicken and cheese. My solution is nachos that are half-loaded for the adults, half plain for the kiddos. (Their loss.)

A few tips: First, use more cheese than you think you need. Next, build nachos in layers—chips + toppings + cheese, then repeat. Finally, leave salsa, guacamole, sour cream, and any other "wet" additions on the side. Putting them on top will make the chips soggy, and soggy nachos are sad nachos.

SMOKY REFRIED PINTOS

MAKE AHEAD!

20 MINUTES · *makes about 2 cups*

IN THE WINTER, I use dried beans, but when the weather heats up, a quick can of beans does the trick.

1 tablespoon olive oil, plus more for drizzling

½ medium yellow onion, chopped

2 garlic cloves, peeled and minced

1 tablespoon tomato paste

1 tablespoon adobo sauce (from chipotle chiles in adobo)

½ teaspoon dried chile powder, like ancho

½ teaspoon ground cumin

½ teaspoon cinnamon

½ teaspoon salt, plus more to taste

15-ounce can pinto beans, drained and rinsed

½ cup canned whole tomatoes in their juice

Heat the oil in a medium skillet over medium heat. Add the onions and cook until softened, 5 minutes. Add the garlic and cook for another minute. Add the tomato paste, the adobo sauce, spices, and salt and cook, stirring, for 1 to 2 minutes. Add the pinto beans and stir to coat. Using your hands, tear and squeeze the tomatoes as you add them to the pan. Stir to combine. Bring to a simmer and cook, stirring occasionally, until mixture has thickened, 10 to 15 minutes. Remove from heat and mash the beans, drizzling in a little water or olive oil as needed to make them creamier. Taste and adjust seasoning, then store in refrigerator.

Nachos with Bits and Bobs

15 MINUTES ACTIVE, 30 MINUTES TOTAL · *serves 4 to 6*

12 ounces sturdy corn chips

1 cup **SMOKY REFRIED PINTOS**

1 cup **GRILLED CHICKEN**, pulled

1 to 2 pieces **GRILLED RED BELL PEPPER**, chopped

½ cup **PICKLED JALAPEÑOS** (pg. 270)

1½ cups shredded monterey jack cheese

1 cup shredded cheddar cheese

½ cup crumbled cotija cheese

2 to 3 radishes, thinly sliced

2 scallions, green parts only, thinly sliced

¼ cup cilantro leaves

¼ cup salsa

1 avocado, mashed and mixed with salt and lime juice to taste

¼ cup plain yogurt or sour cream

1 **Assemble the nachos.** Preheat the oven to 400°F. In a 9x13 inch pan or on a rimmed baking sheet lined with foil, add ⅓ of the chips, top them with ⅓ of the beans, chicken, and peppers, and add a mixture of the cheeses. Repeat 2 more times, finishing with a layer of cheese.

2 **Bake.** Place in the oven until the cheese is melted and bubbling, 10 to 15 minutes.

3 **Finish and serve.** Scatter the radishes, scallions, and cilantro leaves over the nachos and serve with bowls of salsa, mashed avocado, and yogurt or sour cream.

Pasta Salad with Zucchini and Herbs · Roasted Shrimp and Tomato Skewers

40 MINUTES · *serves 4*

THIS DISH IS A FAR CRY from the macaroni-and-mayo concoction that might come to mind when you think of pasta salad. It relies on a zippy vinaigrette, lots of herbs, crunchy pistachios and briny feta to keep it lively. No mayo. I wouldn't do that to you.

As for the shrimp skewers, they're simple, delicious, and kid-friendly (around here, anyway). Keep in mind that shrimp vary in size; I like to buy wild-caught domestic shrimp that are on the larger side for this recipe; look for a count of fifteen to twenty shrimp per pound.

PASTA SALAD WITH ZUCCHINI AND HERBS

1 pound fusilli

LEMON-HONEY VINAIGRETTE

1 cup diced **GRILLED ZUCCHINI**

¼ cup chopped dill

2 tablespoons torn mint leaves

2 tablespoons torn basil leaves

½ cup sheep's milk feta cheese

¼ cup shelled roasted pistachios

ROASTED SHRIMP AND TOMATO SKEWERS

8 metal skewers (if you don't have these, just throw everything on the sheet pan)

24 cherry tomatoes

16 shrimp, shelled and deveined

2 tablespoons olive oil

2 garlic cloves, peeled

3 thyme sprigs

Salt, to taste

Freshly ground black pepper, to taste

1 **Cook the pasta.** Bring a large pot of salted water to a boil and cook the pasta until just al dente. It should be slightly underdone so it can soak up the vinaigrette without getting soggy.

2 **Dress the pasta.** Drain the pasta and rinse with cool water to stop the cooking. When cool, transfer to a large bowl and toss with the vinaigrette.

3 **Assemble the skewers.** Set the oven to 425°F. Thread the skewers so that each has 3 tomatoes and 2 shrimp, alternating. Don't leave any space between the shrimp and tomatoes; squish them as close together as you can without bursting the tomatoes. Place in a shallow baking dish and drizzle with olive oil. Add the garlic, thyme, and a sprinkle of salt and pepper. Toss to coat and refrigerate for 30 minutes or up to 2 days ahead.

4 **Roast the skewers.** Place the skewers on a rimmed baking sheet, pat dry, and roast until the shrimp have just turned pink, about 10 minutes.

5 **Finish the pasta.** While the skewers roast, toss the zucchini, herbs, cheese, and pistachios into the dressed pasta. Stir to combine and season to taste.

6 **Serve.** Remove skewers from oven and serve 2 per person over a heap of the pasta salad.

LEMON-HONEY VINAIGRETTE

MAKE AHEAD!

Juice of 2 lemons (about 6 tablespoons)

1 teaspoon honey

1 small garlic clove, peeled

Salt, to taste

Freshly ground black pepper, to taste

⅓ cup olive oil

Add the lemon juice and honey to a small jar with a lid, secure the lid, and shake until combined. Smash the garlic with the side of a knife, sprinkle a few pinches of salt over it, and mince and smash until a coarse paste forms. Stir the garlic paste into the jar along with a few grinds of pepper. Add the oil, cover, and shake to emulsify.

Panzanella

15 MINUTES ACTIVE, 30 MINUTES TOTAL · *serves 4*

LIKE MANY OF MY SUMMER FAVORITES, this is a simple, adaptable dish that lets good ingredients do the heavy lifting—and it can be made with just about anything you have on hand. The bread is key; a bakery loaf with a dense crust is perfect (even better if it's a day old). Also key: let the dish sit before serving to give the flavors time to mingle. If you're looking for something with a little more heft, torn prosciutto or thinly sliced salami are great additions. (If there's any grilled chicken left, toss it in.)

1 loaf ciabatta, cut into ½-inch slices

4 tablespoons olive oil, divided

Salt, to taste

4 ounces fresh mozzarella, cut into ½-inch cubes

1 medium tomato, cut into ½-inch cubes

3 tablespoons chopped **PICKLED RED ONIONS** (pg. 270)

½ cup chopped **GRILLED RED BELL PEPPERS**

Chicken, salami, or prosciutto (optional)

1 to 2 tablespoons red wine vinegar

Freshly ground black pepper, to taste

1 to 2 cups arugula

¼ cup torn basil leaves

2 tablespoons chopped parsley leaves

1 **Toast the bread.** Heat the oven to 400°F. Toss the sliced bread with 1 tablespoon oil and sprinkle with salt. Toast until bread starts to darken at the edges, about 5 minutes.

2 **Assemble the salad.** While the bread is toasting, mix together the mozzarella, tomato, pickled red onions, and peppers in a large serving bowl. Add chicken, salami, or prosciutto if using. Toss with 2 tablespoons of the oil and the vinegar. Sprinkle with salt and a couple of grinds of pepper.

3 **Add the bread.** When the bread is cool enough to handle, pull it apart into bite-size pieces and add to the salad bowl. Toss to combine and let sit for about 20 minutes.

4 **Finish.** Add the arugula, basil, parsley, and remaining oil and toss to combine. Season to taste with salt and vinegar and serve.

Summer Rolls

30 TO 40 MINUTES TOTAL · *serves 4*

THERE'S NO SHORTAGE OF INGREDIENTS you can put in these summer rolls—carrots, cucumbers, shredded chicken, bean sprouts, enoki mushrooms, or cilantro, just to name a few. Like nori rolls or tacos, this is fun to do with kids because they can choose their fillings and enjoy making a mess (a tasty one though). The volumes for the ingredients below are approximate; the main rule of thumb is not to overstuff the rolls. To get ahead, I'll often blanch the noodles and shrimp earlier in the week.

And since we all know how much kids love to dip their food, whisk together a couple of new dipping sauces. Maybe they'll become your household's new ketchup. I also love to make the peanut sauce (pg. 47) for this meal, but I'm still working on having my kids accept it. It's a process.

RICE WINE DIPPING SAUCE

¼ cup soy sauce

¼ cup rice wine vinegar

1 tablespoon sesame oil

1 garlic clove, peeled and minced

2 scallions, green parts only, chopped

Pinch of brown sugar

SUMMER ROLLS

6 ounces **RICE NOODLES**, cooked

12 rice paper wrappers

24 **COOKED SHRIMP**, cut in half lengthwise if large

12 bibb lettuce leaves

1 cup shredded napa cabbage

1 medium red bell pepper, thinly sliced

1 cup mint leaves

1 cup basil leaves

1 **Make the dipping sauce(s).** Whisk all ingredients together in a small bowl and set aside.

2 **Make the rolls.** Cook the rice noodles according to package directions, drain, and rinse with cool water. Set aside. Have all of the fillings prepped and ready to go. Fill a large bowl with warm water. Submerge a wrapper into the water to soften it (this takes about 10 seconds). Carefully pull it out and lay flat on a clean, damp tea towel (it's important that the towel is damp, otherwise the wrapper will stick).

Arrange 3 to 4 shrimp or shrimp halves in a horizontal row about two-thirds down the wrapper. Place lettuce over the shrimp, followed by a small handful of rice noodles, then a few pieces of cabbage and peppers. Add mint and basil, 2 to 3 leaves of each. Fold the sides of the wrapper in toward the center. Then, starting with the end closest to you, roll it over the filling until you reach the other end. Repeat with remaining wrappers.

3 **Serve** with dipping sauce(s).

GIRL MEETS GRILL

FOR YEARS, GALEN TOOK THE LEAD ON EVERYTHING GRILL-RELATED until one summer evening when he was running late and it was too hot to turn on the oven for whatever we had planned. So I took matters into my own hands, and that night, it took me thirty minutes and practically an entire book of matches to get the thing going. I proceeded to burn the daylights out of some chicken thighs and ended up feeding the kids peanut butter and jelly sandwiches.

I tried again the next night, this time with pizza. Equally humbling. But by day three, I'd taken my neighbor's advice to use a chimney and a long-handled lighter to start the fire, removing a huge barrier to maintaining good morale and having success on the grill.

Grilling, especially over charcoal or wood, is a little unpredictable. Even though I'm usually the one to start the fire and cook the food nowadays, it still feels like practice. And practicing is the only way you'll really get the hang of it. Here are a few things I've learned (about grilling in general and over charcoal or wood specifically):

....

Make two zones. Whether you're grilling over gas or coals, having the heat concentrated on one side lets you sear things over high heat, then finish cooking in the ambient heat. And if your fire flares up, having a cool zone gives you a place to move the food where it won't scorch. When I first started grilling, I'd make a fire in the center, and it was harder to manage the heat. Shunting coals to the side gives you more flexibility to cook things evenly.

Use all of the heat. Let's say you're grilling steak and vegetables. Start with the meat on the hot side, and when you move it to the cooler side, add the vegetables to the spot where the steak was. As the grill cools a bit, you can move the vegetables to the side. Your meal might be cooked, but there's plenty of heat left on the grill. Are there other vegetables in the house that could stand to be cooked? Throw them on the grill and use them in a different dish later in the week. Or grill some fruit, like pineapple or peaches, for a simple dessert.

Move it around. This might be the most fun part of grilling. You really have to watch and respond to what the food needs in terms of heat. If I have a bunch of chicken pieces on the grill, I turn them constantly, switching their placement around depending on how much char the pieces have, which ones need to slow down, and which ones need to speed up. On the grill you can't really set it and forget it (unless you're smoking, but that's another story).

Use a skillet. Once I discovered I could put a skillet on the grill, I never looked back. Almost anything you cook on the stove can be transferred to a skillet on the grill, so you can spend more time outside and keep the kitchen nice and cool.

July

GRILLED BLUEFISH WITH SMOKY EGGPLANT
RELISH • BROCCOLI WITH LEMON AND OLIVES

BLUEFISH CAKES

GRILLED SAUSAGES WITH PEPPERS
AND ONIONS

CHOPPED SALAD WITH
GRILLED CORN AND HALLOUMI

TOMATO GALETTE

IN JULY, when most of the local produce is barreling into farmers' markets, it's time to play! My kids don't always share my passion for salads or grilled vegetables, but they will eat sliced raw stuff by the fistful. I'll often keep some ingredients separate, like green beans and cherry tomatoes, and serve those on a plate with some vinaigrette for dipping, then toss an actual salad together for Galen and me. However the boys get their veg on is fine with me.

LET'S TALK ABOUT BLUEFISH—hands down my favorite finfish. It's briny and meaty with enough brawn to stand up to strong flavors. An average filet weighs about two pounds, so pick up one and use it twice: grill it all, serve half, and reserve the other half for bluefish cakes later in the week. Make sure it's as fresh as you can get it.

And while you're at it, make use of all the grill's heat by throwing on a few ears of corn for a big chopped salad. Slip them into a plastic bag and refrigerate until ready to use. Make a batch of pickled red onions, blanch some green beans and broccoli, and make the dough for a lovely tomato galette later this week. And you're off!

THE BIG COOK

GRILL THE BLUEFISH

BLANCH THE GREEN BEANS
AND BROCCOLI

MAKE THE CORNMEAL PASTRY DOUGH

PICKLE THE RED ONIONS (PG. 270)

MAKE THE LEMON-CHIVE
VINAIGRETTE (PG. 276)

HARD BOIL SOME EGGS (PG. 280)

OTHER WAYS TO GET AHEAD

FORM THE BLUEFISH CAKES THE NIGHT
BEFORE AND STORE IN THE REFRIGERATOR

PREP THE VEGETABLES FOR THE CHOPPED
SALAD (WASH, DRY, AND CHOP ROMAINE;
TRIM SNAP PEAS; GRILL CORN)

Grilled Bluefish with Smoky Eggplant Relish · Broccoli with Lemon and Olives

30 MINUTES ACTIVE, 2½ HOURS TOTAL · *serves 6*

FISH CAN BE TRICKY (also sticky) to grill, leading to frustrating moments when you try to flip a filet. But using a cast iron skillet on the grill makes it easy—offering assurance that nothing will stick or slip through the grates—and gives you great heat and smoky flavor, too.

This meal is a good one for a summer Sunday when you have some time to spare puttering in the kitchen and at the grill. The eggplant relish is the type of thing I make when I ask myself, "What else can go on the grill right now?" I love the slightly charred broccoli with lemon and olives—but if it these directions have you feeling like there's too much to do, try it another night.

GRILLED BLUEFISH

1 2-pound bluefish filet, trimmed of extra fat and skin

1 teaspoon salt

Freshly ground black pepper, to taste

1 tablespoon bacon fat or olive oil

1 teaspoon lemon juice

SMOKY EGGPLANT RELISH

1 eggplant, cut lengthwise into ½-inch slices

1 red onion, quartered and peeled with root end intact

3 tablespoons olive oil, divided

Salt, to taste

3 tablespoons raisins

1 tablespoon capers, drained

1 tablespoon balsamic vinegar

¼ cup chopped parsley

¼ cup chopped mint

BROCCOLI WITH LEMON AND OLIVES

1 head broccoli, cut lengthwise into 1-inch thick slices

1 tablespoon plus 1 teaspoon olive oil

1 garlic clove, peeled

2 tablespoons pitted oil-cured olives, chopped

1 teaspoon lemon zest

1 teaspoon lemon juice

Salt, to taste

Freshly ground black pepper, to taste

TO SERVE

Olive oil, for drizzling

Lemon wedges

Grilled bread (pg. 280)

1 **Light the grill and prep the bluefish.** Pile the coals onto one side (or leave one side of the gas grill off), and place a large cast iron skillet on the grate over the heat. Pat the filet dry and sprinkle both sides with salt and pepper. Cut in half.

2 **Prep the broccoli.** While the grill and the skillet are heating, bring a large pot of salted water to a boil for the broccoli. Blanch for 1 to 2 minutes until the broccoli is bright green, then immediately place in an ice bath. Drain, dry, and put aside. Over low heat, warm 1 tablespoon of oil and the garlic. When the garlic sizzles, turn off the heat and add the olives and lemon zest. Set aside.

3 Grill the bluefish. When the skillet is hot, add the bacon fat or oil and swirl to coat the pan. Place the filets skin-side down in the pan and cook for about 5 minutes, until the fish lifts easily. Flip the fish, move the skillet to the cooler part of the grill, and cover. Cook for another 8 to 10 minutes depending on the thickness of the filet. The fish is done when it flakes easily. Cover 1 filet with foil until ready to serve. Remove the skin from the remaining half, flake the filet, squeeze some lemon juice over top, and reserve in the refrigerator for the Bluefish Cakes.

4 Make the relish. While the bluefish is cooking, rub the eggplant and onion with 1 teaspoon of olive oil each, sprinkle with salt, and place on the hotter side of the grill. Cook for about 3 minutes on each side. Move the vegetables to the cooler side, or turn down heat to medium-low (if you're using a gas grill). Cover and cook for another 5 to 6 minutes, until the eggplant and onions are tender and charred. (The onions might need a little bit longer than the eggplant.) Transfer to a cutting board. When cool enough to handle, dice and place in a small bowl. Stir in the remaining oil, raisins, capers, vinegar, and herbs. Taste and adjust seasoning.

5 Finish the broccoli. Add the blanched broccoli to the skillet and grill for about 2 minutes on each side or until slightly charred, then move to a platter. Remove and discard the garlic clove from the oil, then spoon the olive mixture over the broccoli. Sprinkle with lemon juice and a pinch of salt and pepper. (Psst: this is when you should grill bread.)

6 Finish and serve. Remove the skin from the reserved bluefish filet and divide into 4 servings. Drizzle with olive oil and spoon the relish on or alongside the fish. Serve everything family style with lemon wedges and grilled bread.

WHICH FISH?

OVER THE YEARS, I've spent a good amount of time thinking about the questions we should ask when we're trying to make informed and responsible purchases. And because I grew up in New England, where seafood is a big part of the culture, I pay close attention to the kinds of fish I buy and the social and environmental impact of those purchases.

For me, buying fish is about shopping for what's in season and being flexible. It's not an option for everyone, but I like to buy my fish from vendors who source from regional small boat fishermen year-round. I might have fewer species to choose from, but I'm fine with having a few really good options. Thinking about seafood seasonally means some stuff is a splurge—wild salmon from Alaska in early summer; striped bass through the summer; scallops in the winter—but there are small luxuries I'm happy to fit into the budget. Lots of other species are quite affordable during their seasonal window, like bluefish, redfish, and flounder. Farmed shellfish, like oysters, clams, and mussels, are smart, economical year-round choices, too.

For me, buying fish is about supporting domestic fisheries, especially those closest to home. US fisheries, which are well managed (and improving), can supply our country with all the seafood we need if we diversify the choices that are available to us within our domestic wild fisheries and shellfish aquaculture.

Bluefish Cakes

30 MINUTES · *serves 4*

MAKING FISH CAKES—especially with the bacon fat I've been squirreling away in the back of the fridge—warms my thrifty New Englander's soul. Serve with Stovetop Baked Beans (pg. 278) or my go-to Simple Summer Salad (pg. 275). If you really want to go to town, you can top these with a poached or fried egg.

2 tablespoons bacon fat or canola oil, divided

1 small shallot, peeled and chopped

4 tablespoons chopped parsley

Juice of 1 medium lemon (about 3 tablespoons)

Zest of ½ lemon

1 egg, lightly beaten

1 heaping tablespoon mayonnaise

2 to 3 dashes Tabasco sauce

¾ cup breadcrumbs, divided

1 pound flaked **GRILLED BLUEFISH**

½ teaspoon salt

Freshly ground black pepper, to taste

1 **Make the mixture.** Heat 1 tablespoon of fat in a medium skillet over medium heat. Add the shallot and cook until soft, 2 to 3 minutes. Transfer to a medium bowl and add the parsley, lemon juice and zest, egg, mayonnaise, Tabasco, and ½ cup of breadcrumbs. Stir to combine. Gently fold in the bluefish and season to taste with salt and pepper.

2 **Form the fish cakes.** Using your hands, carefully form the mixture into 4 fish cakes, cover, and refrigerate for at least 20 minutes. The fish cakes can be made up to a day ahead or tightly wrapped and frozen for up to a month.

3 **Fry the fish cakes.** Wipe out the skillet and set it over medium heat. Add the remaining bacon fat or oil. Sprinkle the remaining breadcrumbs onto a small plate; coat the fish cakes in the breadcrumbs on both sides. When the oil shimmers, add the cakes and fry until golden, 3 to 5 minutes on each side.

4 **Serve.** Sprinkle with salt and serve hot with a squeeze of lemon.

Grilled Sausages with Peppers and Onions

30 MINUTES · *serves 4*

DELICIOUS, FAST, VERSATILE, AND FREE OF FUSS, sausage with peppers and onions is one of my favorite weeknight meals. I love baseball, the Red Sox, and Fenway Park, and while I'm more likely to go for peanuts and beer when I'm at a game, I do serve sausages Fenway-style at home: piled into buns with a couple of different mustards (psst: that eggplant relish is really good on sausage, too) and laden with peppers and onions. Next to a big green salad dressed in a Lemon-Chive Vinaigrette (pg. 276), with the game on the radio—it's almost as good as being there.

Tip: I like to double down on the grilled sausages and make way more than we need for dinner. The next night, I'll serve up the leftovers atop flatbreads, like pizza. Summer!

1 tablespoon olive oil, plus more
 for drizzling

2 red bell peppers, cored and sliced

1 medium red onion, sliced

Pinch of salt

1 pound sweet Italian sausages

4 hot dog buns or sub rolls

Basil leaves, for garnish

1 **Light the grill.** Pile the coals onto one side (or leave one side of the gas grill off), clean the grate if needed, and place a medium cast iron skillet on the hot side of the grill.

2 **Grill the peppers and onions.** Add the olive oil to the skillet and, once it shimmers, add the peppers and onions and a pinch of salt. Cover the grill and cook, stirring occasionally, until the vegetables have softened, about 10 minutes.

3 **Grill the sausages.** Move the skillet to the cool side of the grill. Place the sausage on the hot side, cover the grill, and cook until well-charred and cooked through, about another 10 minutes.

4 **Grill the buns.** Brush the buns with a little olive oil and place on the cool side of the grill for 1 to 2 minutes on each side, until warmed through and golden.

5 **Serve.** Place a sausage in each bun and serve the peppers and onions on the side along with the mustards (and the eggplant relish, if you have some left). Tear up the basil leaves and sprinkle them over the top.

Chopped Salad with Grilled Corn and Halloumi

25 MINUTES · *serves 4*

A BIG CHOPPED SALAD is the perfect vehicle to incorporate all the vegetables you impulse-bought at the farmers' market (first sweet corn of the season, I see you). For added heft and interest, I use halloumi, too. This cheese stands up well to high heat, making it the perfect candidate for the grill. Just place the cheese right on the grates, giving it a quick turn to pick up some of that smokiness (too long and it will melt down into the coals). Another option is to get a cast iron skillet nice and hot on the grill or stovetop and crisp up the cheese that way.

2 tablespoons olive oil

1 garlic clove, peeled and smashed

1 teaspoon lemon zest

8 ounces halloumi, cut into ¼-inch slices

¼ cup plus 4 to 5 torn basil leaves

Flaky salt, to taste

Freshly ground black pepper, to taste

2 medium ears corn, shucked

1 medium head romaine, chopped into 1-inch pieces

½ pound green beans, blanched and cut into ½-inch pieces

½ pound snap peas, ends trimmed and thinly sliced

½ cup **PICKLED RED ONIONS**, chopped (pg. 270)

1 medium cucumber, peeled, seeded, and chopped

4 to 5 medium radishes, sliced into half moons

½ pound cherry tomatoes, halved or quartered if large

½ avocado, cut into ¼-inch pieces

¼ cup chopped dill

½ cup **LEMON-CHIVE VINAIGRETTE** (pg. 276)

4 **HARD-BOILED EGGS**, peeled and quartered

1 **Marinate the cheese and prepare the corn.** In a small bowl, toss the oil, garlic, lemon zest, halloumi, and 4 to 5 torn basil leaves with a pinch of salt and a few grinds of pepper. Rub the corn with a drizzle of olive oil. Set aside and light the grill.

2 **Make the salad.** While the grill heats up, combine the romaine, green beans, snap peas, pickled red onions, cucumbers, radishes, tomatoes, avocado, dill, and remaining basil together in a large salad bowl.

3 **Grill the corn and halloumi.** When the grill is hot, clean the grate if necessary and place the corn over indirect heat for about 7 minutes, turning occasionally. Remove and set aside. Place the halloumi over indirect heat for less than 1 minute on each side, just long enough to create grill marks on the cheese and soften it a little. (If using skillet, sear until the cheese starts to pick up some color, then flip.) Remove and set aside. This is the time to grill some bread. (See pg. 280 for tips.)

4 **Finish and serve.** When the corn is cool enough to handle, cut off kernels and add to salad. Drizzle the Lemon-Chive Vinaigrette over the salad and toss to combine. Sprinkle with salt and pepper. Arrange halloumi and hard-boiled egg slices on top and serve.

Rustic Rewards

A GALETTE, A.K.A. A RUSTIC FREE-FORM TART, is an impressive-looking but relatively simple dish. (In other words, just the thing you want in your repertoire.) Once you get the hang of working with the dough, you can riff on the filling to your heart's content. Try it with corn, feta, and herbs, or sautéed apples and onions in the fall.

This summery version calls for oblong Roma tomatoes, which have a lower water content and won't make the galette soggy on the bottom. A light layer of breadcrumbs gives extra insurance against this. While the galette cools, I love to make a quick and refreshing cucumber salad like the one on pg. 273. Win, win.

CORNMEAL PASTRY DOUGH

20 MINUTES · *makes one galette*

1 cup all-purpose flour

½ cup finely ground
cornmeal

1 teaspoon granulated
white sugar

½ teaspoon salt

6 ounces cold
unsalted butter,
cut into chunks

2 to 3 tablespoons
ice water

1 **Mix the ingredients.** In a medium bowl, toss the flour, cornmeal, sugar, and salt together. Scatter the butter chunks over the mixture and use your fingers to smash and press the butter into the flour to create a coarse meal with some coin-sized pieces of butter in the mix. Drizzle the water 1 tablespoon at a time, bringing the dough together with your hands. Add another tablespoon of water if the dough is too dry.

2 **Form the dough.** When the dough forms a rough, shaggy ball, turn it onto a floured work surface and press it into a dome. Using your palm, flatten the dome into a disk, wrap tightly in plastic wrap, and refrigerate for at least 45 minutes or up to 5 days. (Or in the freezer for up to 2 months.)

Tomato Galette

20 MINUTES ACTIVE, 1 HOUR TOTAL · *serves 4*

1 recipe **CORNMEAL
PASTRY DOUGH**

4 Roma tomatoes

1 teaspoon olive oil

2 garlic cloves, peeled
and thinly sliced

Leaves from 3 to 4
thyme sprigs

¼ teaspoon salt, plus
more to taste

Freshly ground black
pepper, to taste

¼ cup coarse
breadcrumbs

1 egg, lightly beaten

1 **Set yourself up.** Heat the oven to 400°F. Line a rimmed baking sheet with parchment paper. Remove the dough from the refrigerator about 10 minutes before you're ready to roll it out. Flour a work surface.

2 **Prep the tomatoes.** Cut an end off of each tomato and gently squeeze the tomatoes over the sink to release a little juice. Cut into ½-inch slices. Place in a bowl with the olive oil, garlic, thyme, salt, and pepper and set aside.

3 **Make the galette.** Roll out the dough into a 9-inch round, dusting with flour as needed to keep it from sticking to the work surface. Transfer to the lined baking sheet. Sprinkle the breadcrumbs over the surface of the dough, leaving a 1-inch border. Arrange the tomatoes in overlapping concentric circles. Evenly distribute the garlic slices among the tomatoes, pour the remaining oil mixture over the top of the filling, and sprinkle with a little extra salt. Fold and crimp the border of the dough around the tomatoes and brush the dough with the beaten egg. Sprinkle with a little salt and pepper.

4 **Bake and serve.** Place in the oven until the crust is golden and the filling is bubbling, 35 to 45 minutes. Cool for at least 20 minutes and serve family style.

Early August

**GRILLED PORK TENDERLOIN · GRILLED PEACHES
& CORN WITH BASIL-CHIVE BUTTER**

PRESSED PORK SANDWICHES

**STUFFED PEPPERS WITH QUINOA,
CORN & MONTEREY JACK**

CLAM & CHORIZO STEW

SUMMER PASTA WITH CALAMARI

BLUEBERRY-PEACH CRISP

THIS MENU REVELS IN THE HOT-WEATHER HARVEST—corn, peaches, tomatoes—while we revel in the heat, the relaxed pace, and the last days of summer before back-to-school season arrives.

MOST OF THE MEALS IN THIS WEEK'S MENU don't require much advance work—all the better to make the most of summer days. Brine the pork tenderloin a couple of days ahead if you can. Since tenderloin is a leaner cut, this quick step helps to keep the meat tender (while infusing it with extra flavor) on the grill. If you can't get to it a day or two in advance, even a few hours in a quick brine goes a long way.

Make a batch of quinoa for the stuffed peppers (double it if you want to have some on hand to throw into salads), and if you know your time will be limited on the weeknights, make the filling and stuff the peppers ahead, too. Just a few simple steps will make night-of dinner prep nice and streamlined (so you can stay a little longer at the beach).

THE BIG COOK

BRINE AND GRILL THE
PORK TENDERLOIN

GRILL THE PEACHES AND CORN

OTHER WAYS TO GET AHEAD

PREP THE STUFFED PEPPERS

A Real Peach

FOR A LONG TIME I eschewed pork tenderloin as being too lean (and dry when cooked) and lacking in flavor. Plus it's a prime cut, which I tend to avoid in favor of cheaper, tastier pieces of the pig (hello, pork shoulder). But as a parent, I value speed more than I used to, and tenderloins are fast-cooking crowd pleasers. And once they're brined and rubbed with spices, they're tender and flavorful, too. Cook two on the grill and save the second one for another meal later in the week—the meat can be flexed into any number of next-day dishes.

Another simple upgrade: make a compound butter (a.k.a. butter mixed with herbs and seasonings). It takes about five minutes and will give the corn a lovely little flavor boost.

TWO-DAY PORK BRINE   MAKE AHEAD!

- 1 gallon water
- ½ cup salt
- ⅓ cup honey
- 2 garlic cloves, peeled and crushed
- 1 tablespoon black peppercorns
- 1 teaspoon red pepper flakes
- 1 teaspoon fennel seeds
- 2 1-pound pork tenderloins

Brine the pork. At least 1 hour before cooking (and up to 2 days in advance), prepare the brine. In a large pot, combine the water, salt, honey, garlic, peppercorns, and fennel seeds and stir until dissolved. Trim any excess fat or skin from the pork, then add the pork to the pot. Cover and refrigerate until ready to grill.

Grilled Pork Tenderloin • Grilled Peaches & Corn with Basil-Chive Butter

45 MINUTES · *serves 4*

BASIL-CHIVE BUTTER

8 tablespoons unsalted butter, at room temperature

2 tablespoons chopped basil leaves

2 tablespoons chopped chives

Flaky salt, like Maldon

PORK TENDERLOIN

2 tablespoons brown sugar

1 teaspoon cumin seeds, toasted and ground

½ teaspoon cinnamon

½ teaspoon salt

¼ teaspoon freshly ground black pepper

2 1-pound **PORK TENDERLOINS**, brined

GRILLED CORN & PEACHES

4 ears corn, shucked

Olive oil

2 peaches, halved and pitted

1 teaspoon balsamic vinegar

Pinch of brown sugar

Flaky salt, to taste

Freshly ground black pepper, to taste

1 **Make the basil-chive butter.** In a small bowl, use a fork to mash the butter. Add the basil, chives, and a few fat pinches of salt and stir to combine. Use a spatula to scrape the butter into a mound, then transfer to a length of plastic wrap and roll into a log. Wrap the butter and refrigerate until ready to use.

2 **Light the grill.** If using charcoal, pile the coals onto one side of the grill. When they burn down, spread them out into an even pile on that side. If using a gas grill, light one side to high, cover, and let it heat up. Set the other side to low.

3 **Make the dry rub.** Mix together all the ingredients in a small bowl. Remove the pork from the brine and pat dry, then apply the rub.

4 **Grill the pork.** Place pork on the grill, cover, and sear for 4 to 5 minutes on each side. Move the pork to the cool side of the grill, cover, and cook for another 8 to 10 minutes until the temperature reaches 145°F for medium-rare. Remove from the grill, cover with foil, and rest at least 10 minutes before slicing, reserving 1 tenderloin for a later meal.

5 **Grill the corn.** Add the corn to the hot side of the grill. Brush with oil, turning occasionally. Grill for about 10 minutes, then transfer to a platter and spread with compound butter.

6 **Grill the peaches.** Brush the peaches with oil, place them cut-side down on the hot side of the grill, and cook for 3 to 4 minutes (long enough to develop grill marks). Transfer to the cooler side and cook, cut-side up, 5 minutes more. (Careful not to burn them.) Remove from grill and transfer to a bowl. Toss with a drizzle of olive oil and vinegar. Add a pinch of brown sugar, salt, and pepper.

7 **Finish and serve.** Thinly slice the pork and arrange on a platter with the peaches and grilled corn.

Pressed Pork Sandwiches

20 MINUTES ACTIVE, ABOUT 1½ HOURS TOTAL (INCLUDES SITTING TIME) · *serves 4*

I LIKE TO MAKE THIS SANDWICH on one big loaf of bread, then wrap it in plastic wrap and let it sit a bit until I'm ready to press and serve it. It's easier than making four or six sandwiches, and more fun, too. This is a good candidate to bring hiking or camping; it keeps well, tastes great at room temperature, and does even better warmed and pressed over a fire.

1 loaf ciabatta, halved horizontally

2 tablespoons olive oil, plus 1 teaspoon, divided

¼ cup apple butter

¼ cup dijon mustard

Salt, to taste

12 to 16 ounces thinly sliced **GRILLED PORK TENDERLOIN**

1 cup arugula

Splash of red wine vinegar

4 to 6 ounces thinly sliced cheddar cheese

1 **Prepare the bread.** Place the bread on a work surface cut-side up and remove some of the inside dough from both the top and bottom. Drizzle both pieces of bread with 1 tablespoon olive oil. Spread the apple butter on one piece and the mustard on the other. Sprinkle with salt.

2 **Assemble the sandwich.** Layer the pork onto the bottom piece of bread. Toss the arugula in a small bowl with 1 teaspoon olive oil and a splash of vinegar. Place the arugula on top of the pork and top with the cheese. Place the top piece of bread onto the sandwich and press down. Wrap tightly in plastic wrap until ready to serve (waiting an hour is good, but if you only have 30 minutes that's cool, too.)

3 **Press the sandwich.** To heat the sandwich, brush the bread with the remaining tablespoon of olive oil and place in a large skillet over medium heat. Cover with another skillet and cook, pressing down on the top skillet occasionally and flipping the sandwich occasionally, until the filling is warm, the cheese is melted, and the crust is crisp, about 20 minutes. Cut into slices and serve.

Stuffed Peppers with Quinoa, Corn & Monterey Jack

15 MINUTES ACTIVE, 40 MINUTES TOTAL · *serves 4*

THESE STUFFED PEPPERS HAVE MAKE-AHEAD POTENTIAL, but they also come together pretty quickly from start to finish, especially if you've cooked a batch of quinoa in advance. Cubing the cheese (rather than shredding it) gives the finished product a little extra gooey factor—never a bad thing in my opinion. I serve these with a simple salad on the side (see pg. 275).

4 medium poblano peppers or 8 small mild peppers, like cubanelles

1 cup corn kernels (about 2 medium ears)

½ cup quinoa

½ teaspoon salt, plus more to taste

3 scallions, dark and light green parts, chopped

4 ounces monterey jack cheese, cut into ¼-inch cubes

½ teaspoon sweet paprika

Freshly ground black pepper, to taste

Chopped cilantro

Lime wedges

1 **Heat the oven to 400°F.** Place a large skillet over medium-high heat. When it's hot, add the peppers and char them, turning frequently, until they've softened all over and are blackened in spots. Set aside until cool enough to handle, then make a vertical slit down the center of each pepper. Remove and discard the seeds.

2 **Make the stuffing.** Combine the corn, quinoa, scallions, cheese, and paprika in a small bowl. Season to taste with salt and pepper. Stuff the filling into the peppers. If you are serving these later in the week, store tightly covered until ready to bake.

3 **Finish and serve.** Bake until the cheese is bubbling, 20 to 25 minutes. Serve hot and garnish with cilantro and lime.

Clam & Chorizo Stew

15 MINUTES ACTIVE, 30 MINUTES TOTAL · *serves 4 to 6*

THIS IS ACTUALLY A YEAR-ROUND DISH FOR US. In winter I use canned tomatoes and it's a total delight. But come summer, I use diced fresh tomatoes and cook this on the grill so it gets a little smoky. Oh man, it's good. Just be ready to move the pan around between direct and indirect heat to keep the ingredients cooking at the right temp.

2 pounds littleneck clams

2 tablespoons olive oil

12 ounces chorizo, cut into ¼-inch half moons

1 yellow onion, chopped

Salt, to taste

½ medium fennel bulb, sliced

3 to 4 garlic cloves, peeled and chopped

1½ cups diced tomatoes

½ cup white wine

TO SERVE

Chopped parsley

Crusty or grilled bread

1 **Soak the clams.** Place the clams in a pot, cover with cool water, and let them soak for at least 20 minutes. This helps release some of the sand that can make them gritty. Set a colander in the sink and transfer the clams, a few at a time, to the colander, then rinse again.

2 **Light the grill.** If using charcoal, pile the coals onto one side of the grill. When they burn down, spread them out into an even pile on that side. If using a gas grill, light one side to hot, cover, and let it heat up. Set the other side to low.

3 **Cook the chorizo and aromatics.** Place a dutch oven on the grill over direct heat and add the olive oil. Add the chorizo and cook for 2 minutes on each side, until lightly browned. Remove from the pot and set aside. Move the pot to the cooler side of the grill and add the onions and a pinch of salt and cook, stirring, until softened, 2 to 3 minutes. Add the fennel and cook, stirring, for another 4 to 5 minutes. Add the garlic and another pinch of salt, stir to combine, and cook for about 1 minute.

4 **Make the broth.** Add the tomatoes. Cook, stirring, until they start to break down, about 5 minutes. Add the wine and bring to a simmer.

5 **Add the clams.** Cover the pot, move it back over the direct heat, and cook until all of the clams have opened, 10 to 15 minutes. Return the chorizo to the pot until warmed through.

6 **Finish and serve.** Sprinkle stew with parsley. Serve with grilled bread (pg. 280) or a big bowl of buttered pasta or rice.

Summary Pasta with Calamari

35 MINUTES · *serves 4 to 6*

SOMETIMES ONLY A BOWL OF PASTA WILL DO—even in the summertime. This dish hits so many of my favorite notes: it's garlicky, zippy with (one entire) lemon, and dotted with intensely sweet little tomatoes. Plus it involves an inexpensive and novel seafood species that one of my sons devours, which seals the deal for me. Squid strikes me as a convenience food of sorts. It's relatively inexpensive and it cooks quickly—once you gather and prep the ingredients, this meal comes together fast.

1 pound fusilli

3 tablespoons olive oil, divided

1 lemon, halved and seeded

1 large garlic clove, minced

1 small zucchini, diced

2 pounds calamari (tubes and tentacles), tubes sliced into ½-inch rings

½ pint cherry tomatoes, halved if large

1 to 2 tablespoons unsalted butter, at room temperature

Salt, to taste

Freshly ground black pepper, to taste

¼ cup torn basil leaves

1 **Cook the pasta according to package directions.** Reserve 1 cup pasta water, drain the pasta, toss with 1 tablespoon olive oil, and set aside.

2 **Start the sauce.** Dice a half lemon, rind and pulp, making sure to remove any seeds. Pour 2 tablespoons olive oil into a large sauté pan over medium heat. When the oil shimmers, add the garlic and the diced lemon and cook, stirring, until the lemon has softened, about 3 minutes. Add the zucchini and cook, stirring, until soft, 4 to 5 minutes.

3 **Add the calamari.** Cook, stirring, until it just starts to turn firm and opaque, about 3 minutes. Add the cherry tomatoes and cook until they soften and collapse.

4 **Add the pasta.** Splash in some reserved pasta water. Stir in the butter and some juice from remaining half lemon and continue to cook, adding more pasta water as needed, until the butter has emulsified with the cooking liquid in the pan and the pasta is glossy and coated in sauce. Season with salt and pepper.

5 **Finish and serve.** Sprinkle pasta with basil and serve.

FRUIT PICKING

EVERY YEAR, WE TAKE THE KIDS TO NEARBY ORCHARDS and fruit farms to do the U-Pick thing. I used to try to bring home as much as humanly possible—and then attempt to bake treats, freeze bags of fruit, and put up preserves. All on the same day. Whew.

Over the years, I've learned to temper my ambitions. Sure, it's satisfying to have a freezer full of blueberries and a pantry full of peach jam, but it's also nice to spend a leisurely day picking fruit and playing in the orchard without any forced marches or meltdowns.

I still aspire to go out and gather fruit throughout our short season: strawberries in June, blueberries in July, peaches and plums in August, and apples in October. Because it's thrilling to crack open strawberry preserves on Christmas morning and spread it on fancy toast. Or to pull fruit from the freezer in February and make a just-like-summer fruit crisp. Here's a super simple one you can make after a day of picking or with your freezer stash when you need a hit of summer's sweetness. If you're working with frozen fruit, don't thaw it first.

Blueberry-Peach Crisp

20 MINUTES ACTIVE, ABOUT AN HOUR TOTAL · *serves 6 to 8*

TOPPING

- ½ cup all-purpose flour
- ½ cup light brown sugar
- ½ cup rolled oats
- ¼ cup almonds, chopped
- ½ teaspoon freshly grated nutmeg
- ½ teaspoon ground ginger
- Pinch of salt
- ½ stick unsalted butter, chilled

FILLING

- 4 to 5 medium peaches, peeled, pitted, and sliced
- 2 cups blueberries
- 1 tablespoon freshly grated ginger
- 1 to 2 tablespoons lemon juice
- ½ cup granulated sugar
- 1 tablespoon all-purpose flour

1 **Make the topping.** Heat the oven to 375°F. In a medium bowl, toss all of the ingredients together, except for the butter. Cut the butter into chunks and toss with the dry ingredients, working the butter with your fingers to give the mixture a pebbly texture while leaving some bigger chunks of butter in there. Set aside.

2 **Make the filling.** Toss the peaches, blueberries, ginger, lemon juice, sugar, and flour together in a large bowl. Transfer to a 9x9 inch baking dish and place on a sheet pan.

3 **Bake.** Sprinkle the topping over the fruit and bake until the fruit is bubbling and the topping is browned, about 45 minutes. Cool for at least 10 minutes before serving.

Late August

STUFFED TOMATOES

LAMB AND VEGETABLE KEBABS • SPICED BULGUR

BLACK-EYED PEA BURGERS

BLTS

SESAME STRIPED BASS • GINGER-CUCUMBER SALAD

IT'S TOMATO TIME! One of my desert island foods, in-season tomatoes hitch a ride with practically every meal I eat for the better part of August. (Breakfast included. If you've never eaten sliced, salted tomatoes on peanut butter toast, don't knock it 'til you try it. It's savory perfection.) Even if they're not central to the meal, like with stuffed tomatoes or BLTs, they make their way onto our plates regardless—usually just sliced and sprinkled with salt, because that's the best way.

COOKING THIS TIME OF YEAR is really more like assembling: you figure out a streamlined summer repertoire, prep as much as you can ahead of time, and serve it up with minimum fuss. By the time fall rolls around, I'll be ready for real cooking again, but for now, I'm content to let the seasonal produce do the heavy lifting. I mean, a big pile of corn and a BLT with lettuce and tomatoes from the garden is good eating.

But this is a cookbook, not a sandwich manual, so I've included a couple of recipes that involve a little more than putting delicious things on bread. To get ahead, make a batch of spiced bulgur—some to stuff into tomatoes, the rest to serve with the kebabs. You can also make the black-eyed pea burgers and some pickled red onions (a workhorse item if ever there was one) ahead of time, and clean and dry some lettuce. All these little things will add up to an easy late summer week.

THE BIG COOK

MAKE A BATCH OF SPICED BULGUR

PREP THE BLACK-EYED PEA BURGERS

OTHER WAYS TO GET AHEAD

MARINATE THE LAMB IN ADVANCE

PICKLE THE RED ONIONS (PG. 270)

With a Kick

AS GRAINS GO, BULGUR IS A SUMMER FAVORITE. I pour hot water over the grains, cover, and let it sit while I go about my business. Once the liquid is absorbed, I throw in a ton of chopped herbs (as many varieties as I have around), plus a few spices and whatever else works with the meal's flavors.

When I'm prepping in advance, I cook and season the bulgur, but wait to add the chopped herbs until just before serving to keep them fresh and vibrant. You can serve this warm or at room temperature—it's great either way.

SPICED BULGUR   MAKE AHEAD!

10 MINUTES ACTIVE, 40 MINUTES TOTAL · *makes 4 cups*

1½ cups dry bulgur

2 cups water or stock

3 tablespoons olive oil

1 teaspoon ground sumac

½ teaspoon ground cumin

Zest from one lemon

1 to 2 tablespoons lemon juice

½ teaspoon salt

½ teaspoon Urfa or Aleppo pepper
  (or another mild ground chile)

¼ cup torn mint leaves

¼ cup chopped parsley

¼ cup chopped dill

1 **Cook the bulgur.** Place the bulgur in a medium bowl. Bring the water or stock to a boil and pour the boiling liquid over the bulgur. Cover and let sit for about 30 minutes. Strain through a sieve, pressing out any liquid.

2 **Season.** Return to the bowl and stir in the olive oil, sumac, cumin, lemon zest and juice, salt, and pepper. Set aside until ready to serve. (Use half of the bulgur alongside kebabs and reserve the rest for stuffed tomatoes.)

3 **Finish.** Just before serving, add the chopped herbs and toss to combine. Season to taste.

Stuffed Tomatoes

15 MINUTES ACTIVE, 45 MINUTES TOTAL · *serves 4*

THESE SUPER SAVORY TOMATOES are a solid meatless main course for dinner or lunch. Serve them with a chopped romaine salad (pg. 275) or steamed corn to keep things vegetarian, or use them as a side with grilled steak or lamb. So good.

A note about timing: These firm up as they rest, so if you have time to make them an hour ahead, do it—then finish them up with a sprinkle of breadcrumbs and a few minutes under the broiler before serving.

2 tablespoons olive oil

½ small yellow onion, chopped

2 teaspoons tomato paste

1½ cups **SPICED BULGUR**

2 teaspoons pomegranate molasses

2 to 3 tablespoons chopped toasted walnuts or shelled pistachios

¼ cup sheep's milk feta, crumbled

4 large beefsteak tomatoes

Salt, to taste

1 to 2 tablespoons breadcrumbs

1 **Make the stuffing.** Heat the oven to 350°F. In a medium skillet, heat the olive oil over medium heat. When it's warm, add the onions and cook, stirring, for 3 to 4 minutes, until the onion has started to soften. Add the tomato paste and cook, stirring, for another 2 to 3 minutes. Scrape the onion mixture into a bowl with the spiced bulgur and stir to combine. Stir in the pomegranate molasses, nuts, and feta, and season to taste.

2 **Prep the tomatoes.** Use a paring knife to core the tomatoes (working about ½ inch from the stem) and use a spoon to remove as much of the pulp and seeds as possible without breaking the skin.

3 **Stuff the tomatoes.** Sprinkle the insides of the tomatoes with salt. Dividing the filling evenly, stuff the tomatoes. Replace the tops on each.

4 **Bake the tomatoes.** Place tomatoes in a shallow baking dish and bake until soft and a little wrinkly, about 25 to 30 minutes. Remove and discard the tops, sprinkle the breadcrumbs over the tomatoes, and place under the broiler until toasty and browned, about 3 minutes. Cool for 5 minutes. Serve hot or at room temperature.

Lamb and Vegetable Kebabs · Spiced Bulgur

30 MINUTES ACTIVE, 1 HOUR TOTAL · *serves 4 to 6*

ONE OF MY FAVORITE COOKBOOKS is *The New Book of Middle Eastern Food* by Claudia Roden. Whenever I pick up this book I learn something, whether it's a bit of history or a simple technique for amplifying flavor. That's the case for this lamb marinade, which involves puréeing a whole onion with olive oil and seasoning—a simple move that adds big flavor.

1 small yellow onion

¼ cup plus one teaspoon olive oil

1 teaspoon salt

2 pounds boned lamb leg

2 garlic cloves, peeled and
smashed

4 to 5 mint sprigs

4 to 5 marjoram or oregano
sprigs (optional)

Freshly ground black pepper,
to taste

1 medium red onion, cut in half
crosswise (through the center
of the onion) and ends removed

1 red bell pepper, seeded and cut
into 1-inch chunks

12 to 14 metal or wood skewers (if
using wood, soak in water for 15
to 30 minutes in advance)

1 ½ cups **SPICED BULGUR**

TO SERVE

Herby Yogurt Sauce (pg. 277)

Parsley Pesto (pg. 75)

1 **Marinate the lamb.** Cut the yellow onion into chunks and purée in a blender. Add the ¼ cup oil and the salt and blend until combined. Cut the lamb into 1-inch pieces and toss in a shallow baking dish with the onion mixture, garlic, herbs, and a few grinds of pepper. Marinate for at least 30 minutes or overnight in the fridge.

2 **Assemble the vegetable skewers.** Light the grill and pile the coals onto one side (or set a gas grill to high heat on one side and low on the other). Set the red onion halves cut-side down and cut each half into 4 to 8 pieces depending on the size of the onion. The chunks should be about the same size as the peppers. Thread 6 to 8 skewers with alternating pieces of onion and pepper. Place skewers in a shallow dish and toss with the remaining teaspoon olive oil and a pinch of salt and pepper.

3 **Assemble the lamb skewers.** Remove the lamb from the marinade and thread onto 6 skewers.

4 **Grill!** Grill the vegetable skewers for about 2 minutes on each side, then move them to the cool side of the grill. Grill the lamb kebabs for 4 to 5 minutes on each side. They should be well-seared on the outside but still pink within. Keep an eye on the vegetables while the lamb is cooking to make sure they're not over (or under) cooking. Transfer the lamb and vegetables to a platter and drizzle with a little more olive oil. Serve with Spiced Bulgur, Herby Yogurt Sauce, Parsley Pesto, and flatbread.

A Running List

ONE OF THE REASONS I GOT RELIGIOUS about planning out our meals was to fill a creative need and make space to come up with new ideas. Without carving out the time to plan, my repertoire narrowed to the handful of things that first came to mind when answering the big question: *what's for dinner?* Now that I've been doing it for a few years, I have running lists of meals that are easy or more ambitious; dinners that hit a kiddo homerun and those that are a tougher sell; dishes that fit certain themed nights and those that might only come out once a season.

These smoky, savory veggie burgers are on a bunch of running lists. They're simple, kid-friendly, meatless, and economical (they're a familiar dish in the weeks when we're tightening the budget). And they're so tasty that they're a regular feature on the most important list of all: the one on the kitchen chalkboard.

BLACK-EYED PEA BURGERS

MAKE AHEAD!

30 MINUTES · *serves 4*

1 tablespoon olive oil

1 small yellow onion, chopped

3 garlic cloves, peeled and chopped

1 small red bell pepper, chopped

1 tablespoon tomato paste

½ teaspoon smoked paprika

2 cups cooked black-eyed peas

Splash of red wine vinegar

1 egg

1 cup breadcrumbs, divided

1 teaspoon salt

2 to 3 tablespoons chopped parsley

1 to 2 tablespoon chopped chives

Canola oil, for frying

TO SERVE

4 sesame seed buns

Lettuce leaves

PICKLED RED ONIONS (pg. 270)

Herby Yogurt Sauce (pg. 277)

1 **Make the mixture.** Heat the olive oil in a medium skillet over medium heat. Add the onions and cook, stirring, until they soften, 2 to 3 minutes. Add the garlic and the pepper and cook, stirring, for another 3 to 4 minutes. Add the tomato paste and paprika and cook, stirring, for another 1 to 2 minutes, then stir in the black-eyed peas.

When the black-eyed peas are warmed through, add the vinegar, remove from heat, transfer to a bowl, and mash the mixture with a fork until blended, leaving it a little chunky for texture. Add the egg, half of the breadcrumbs, salt, and herbs, mix until combined, and season to taste.

2 **Make the burger patties.** Form the mixture into 4 round patties and refrigerate for at least 15 minutes or until ready to cook. These keep in the refrigerator for up to 5 days.

3 **Ready to fry.** Place the remaining breadcrumbs on a plate and remove burger patties from the refrigerator. Heat 2 to 3 tablespoons of canola oil in a large skillet over medium heat. Dip each side of the burgers in the breadcrumbs. Fry for 3 to 4 minutes or until dark golden, then flip, and cook the other side.

4 **Assemble.** Toast the buns. Place a patty on each and top with the yogurt sauce, pickled red onions, and lettuce. (My kids like to prepare theirs just like a regular burger with ketchup, mustard, and pickles.)

LATE AUGUST

BLTs

20 MINUTES · *serves 4*

I DEBATED WHETHER THIS BOOK NEEDED a recipe for a BLT since most people have their own favorite way of making them. But my older boy was five before it occurred to me that we could eat these for dinner—and joy, it's something both kids actually like. A good sandwich is a great dinner, especially when it involves bacon and summer tomatoes.

If I'm in the mood, I'll fry the bread lightly in the fat that's rendered from the bacon—smoky, rich, and delicious. Served with steamed corn or the Green Bean Salad on pg. 273, it's truly the perfect summer meal.

¼ cup mayonnaise

1½ teaspoons smoked paprika

12 to 16 pieces bacon

8 slices of your favorite white sandwich bread

Salt, to taste

Freshly ground black pepper, to taste

4 to 8 lettuce leaves (I like bibb)

2 to 3 ripe tomatoes, thickly sliced

Mix the mayonnaise and paprika in a small bowl and set aside. Place the bacon in a large skillet over medium-low heat and cook until it's to your liking (keep the heat on the low side). I like it pretty crisp, so I'll cook it for about 10 minutes total. Transfer to a paper towel-lined plate to drain.

Toast the bread, then spread each piece with a bit of mayonnaise. Sprinkle with salt and pepper. Layer the bacon, lettuce, and tomato between the bread. Cut in half and serve.

Sesame Striped Bass · Ginger-Cucumber Salad

20 MINUTES ACTIVE, 50 MINUTES TOTAL · *serves 4*

STRIPED BASS IS ANOTHER ALL-TIME FAVORITE FISH and a rare treat in our house, unless I'm lucky enough to snag some from a friend who had a particularly good fishing day.

This fresh and crunchy cucumber salad is inspired by Boston-area chef Steve Johnson's submission to my first cookbook, *The Boston Homegrown Cookbook*. Start the salad, steam some rice (pg. 280 for tips), and soon you'll have a special weeknight meal on your table.

GINGER-CUCUMBER SALAD

½ small red onion, peeled and thinly sliced

½ cup lime juice (about 4 to 5 limes)

1 tablespoon granulated sugar

1 teaspoon salt

1 teaspoon fish sauce

1 large cucumber

2 to 3 tablespoons chopped pickled ginger

2 tablespoons chopped mint

2 tablespoons chopped cilantro

SESAME STRIPED BASS

4 6-ounce striped bass filets, skin on

Salt, to taste

2 to 3 tablespoons canola oil

1 to 2 teaspoons sesame oil

4 tablespoons toasted sesame seeds

1 lime

1 **Marinate the onions.** Anywhere from 30 minutes to 2 hours before you cook the fish, toss the onions with the lime juice, sugar, salt, and fish sauce in a small bowl.

2 **Prep the fish.** Heat the oven to 450°F. Pat the filets dry, then sprinkle both sides with salt.

3 **Sear the fish.** Heat a large skillet over high heat for about 3 minutes. Add the oil and when it's hot, place the fish, skin-side down in the skillet and sear for about 3 minutes, until it starts to turn opaque on the side touching the pan (turn heat to medium-high if it starts to get smoky). With the fish still skin-side down, transfer to the oven and roast for 9 to 12 minutes, until the fish is cooked through (registering about 140°F on a meat thermometer) and flakes easily with a fork. Remove from oven and immediately drizzle each filet with sesame oil and sprinkle with sesame seeds. Give each filet a little squirt of lime juice and let it rest while you finish up the salad.

4 **Finish the salad.** Peel and seed the cucumber, then cut into half moons. Toss with the marinated onions and pickled ginger. Just before serving, add the mint and cilantro.

5 **Serve.** Serve the fish and salad with steamed rice and extra lime wedges.

COOKING WHILE CAMPING

RECENTLY, WE'VE STARTED TO DO OUR FAIR SHARE of camping. We haven't worked our way up to backpacking yet—we'll get there at some point—but for now we're happy packing up a car or a boat and getting ourselves to a site where we can pitch a tent and explore the area around us. It's incredibly freeing (especially for the kids) to not have any walls around us, except for those of a tent at night. No cell service is a bonus, too.

As for me, I've gotten a little addicted to the challenge of cooking outside over a fire. First there's the menu planning (clearly my favorite thing, even more so when it's for an occasion), the packing, and then the prep—which ideally can be done in a small space with one knife—and finally the cooking itself. It's an exercise in creativity and economy, often serving up pretty tasty (and sometimes even elegant) food.

Here are a few tips for planning, packing, and preparing a great meal at your campsite:

Keep it together: Pots, pans, utensils, and pantry items like salt and olive oil should all be stored together. When you're packing up, you won't have to scour the kitchen, pantry, and basement for your cooking kit.

Think through the details: What do you want to make? What kind of equipment do you need? Can you use the same equipment again for the morning meal? What's the cooking situation like where you're heading?

Make a list and check it (multiple times): Make sure you have the right equipment and ingredients for whatever you're planning to cook. I like to avoid a trip to the store once I've set up camp.

Most perishable first: There's no reason why you shouldn't cook fish or chicken when camping, but plan for it. Cook the most delicate or perishable things on your first night, before the ice has a chance to melt.

Prep ahead: Marinate meat or vegetables ahead of time and pack them into resealable bags that can lie flat in your cooler.

Balance your effort: Not every meal needs to be an all-out experience. A hot breakfast is special, but yogurt and granola works just as well, as do sandwiches for dinner.

Early September

**GRILLED FLANK STEAK WITH
RED PEPPER-WALNUT SAUCE • DRESSED GREENS**

**GRILLED ROMAINE SALAD WITH STEAK
AND SLICED TOMATOES**

GRILLED VEGETABLE PANINI

COLD SOBA NOODLE SALAD

ZUCCHINI FRITTERS

CHOCOLATE-BUCKWHEAT COOKIES

BOSTON CHEF GORDON HAMERSLEY once remarked to me that the reason food and cooking in New England is so unique is because we have six seasons, not four. "Look at the difference between September and November," he said. It's true, and when summer and fall collide and you can find tomatoes, eggplant, and corn alongside squash and apples at the farmers' market, it's exhilarating (it's the little things, friends). Do we grill, braise, roast, or eat it raw? Yes. Yes we do.

Experience has taught me that reentry into the school year is not the time to dive into big kitchen projects—we need to get outside while the getting's good. So this week's menu tries to hit that sweet spot with lots of late summer produce and simple dishes that come together quickly.

THIS WEEK'S MENU KEEPS ADVANCE PREP TO A MINIMUM with most of it happening on the grill. When I want to streamline my prep even further, I think through how I can use my time and sequence my activity most efficiently.

Here's how I do it: put peppers on the grill first and make vinaigrette while they cook. Then grill the steak and remaining vegetables while the peppers cool (note to fellow charcoal enthusiasts: make a big fire). While the steak is on the grill, pull together the ingredients for the Red Pepper-Walnut Sauce and salad. Once the peppers have cooled enough to remove their skins, make the sauce. While the steak rests, have one of the kids toss together a salad right before serving the meal.

After dinner, take stock. You have Red Pepper-Walnut Sauce and grilled vegetables at the ready for a panini feast on any given busy evening, and a pound of sliced flank steak that you can toss into a grilled romaine salad for another night's dinner, too. All that for a busy hour of weekend prep. Well done!

THE BIG COOK

GRILL THE RED PEPPERS, EGGPLANT, ZUCCHINI AND FLANK STEAK

MAKE THE RED PEPPER-WALNUT SAUCE

MAKE THE HONEY-LIME DRESSING

OTHER WAYS TO GET AHEAD

COOK AND STORE THE SOBA NOODLES

WASH AND STORE THE LETTUCE AND HERBS

Fire it Up

SOMEWHERE BETWEEN a muhammara and a romesco sauce, you'll want this spread in your kitchen all the time—to smear on toast, spoon over meat or fish, stir into eggs, or scoop up with fresh vegetables. I love the smoky taste the grill lends to the peppers here, but you can also rely on your oven: simply broil the peppers for 8 to 10 minutes and proceed.

Flank steaks usually run about two pounds, so I tend to buy a whole one and use it for two meals. I find that slicing the meat before serving helps me control the portion sizes, making it easier to meet that goal. Reserve the remaining sliced steak for the romaine salad later in the week.

Grilled Flank Steak with Red Pepper-Walnut Sauce • Dressed Greens

30 MINUTES · *serves 4*

1 2-pound flank steak

1 to 2 teaspoons salt

2 sprigs oregano

DRESSED GREENS

4 cups mixed greens

1 cup basil leaves, torn into 1-inch pieces

2 tablespoons olive oil

1 tomato, cut into ½-inch slices

¼ cup chopped toasted almonds

1 tablespoon white wine vinegar

Salt, to taste

Freshly ground black pepper, to taste

2 ounces sheep's milk feta, crumbled

TO SERVE

½ cup **RED PEPPER-WALNUT SAUCE**

Oregano leaves

1 **Grill the steak.** Light a charcoal or gas grill to high heat on one side (keep the other side on low). Pat the steak dry and rub with salt. Place the steak over the hottest part and grill for 3 to 4 minutes. Flip and cook for another 3 minutes, then move to a cooler spot on the grill, cover, and cook for an additional 2 to 3 minutes. For medium-rare steak, the interior temperature should be about 125°F; for medium, about 135°F. Transfer the steak to a cutting board and cover with foil to rest for 10 minutes. Reserve half for dinner later in the week.

2 **Make the salad.** Place the mixed greens and basil in a large salad bowl and toss with olive oil. Add the tomato, almonds, and vinegar and toss to combine. Season to taste with salt and pepper. Sprinkle the salad with crumbled feta.

3 **Serve.** Thinly slice the steak and arrange on plates with a dollop of the Red Pepper-Walnut Sauce and a sprinkle of torn oregano leaves. Serve the salad alongside.

RED PEPPER-WALNUT SAUCE

MAKE AHEAD!

10 MINUTES · *makes 2 cups*

1 cup toasted walnuts, skins removed

4 grilled or broiled **RED BELL PEPPERS**, skins and seeds removed (see pg. 272)

1 tablespoon tomato paste

1 garlic clove, chopped

Juice of 1 lemon

2 tablespoons olive oil, divided

½ teaspoon pomegranate molasses (optional, or substitute a splash of balsamic vinegar and a ½ teaspoon of brown sugar)

¼ teaspoon salt, plus more to taste

¼ teaspoon smoked paprika, plus more to taste

⅛ teaspoon ground Aleppo pepper, plus more to taste

Coarsely chop the walnuts. Put the roasted peppers in a food processor with the chopped walnuts, tomato paste, garlic, lemon juice, and remaining 1 tablespoon of olive oil. Purée until smooth, transfer to a bowl, and stir in the pomegranate molasses, salt, paprika, and Aleppo pepper. Season to taste. This sauce will keep in the refrigerator for 5 to 7 days.

All Dressed Up

CHEF BARRY MAIDEN submitted a similar salad recipe for a story I worked on recently. I couldn't stop making it for months. Here's a riff on Maiden's grilled romaine, with some steak and tomatoes added for main-course heft.

HONEY-LIME DRESSING

MAKE AHEAD!

5 MINUTES · *makes about 1 cup*

¼ cup fresh lime juice (from 2 or 3 limes)

2 tablespoons honey

1 teaspoon dijon mustard

1 small garlic clove, peeled and finely grated

¼ teaspoon ground cumin

½ teaspoon salt

½ teaspoon freshly ground black pepper

¼ cup olive oil

¼ cup grapeseed or canola oil

Combine the lime juice, honey, mustard, garlic, cumin, salt, and pepper in a jar with a tight-fitting lid. Secure the lid and shake until well combined. Add the oils and shake until the dressing has emulsified. This vinaigrette will keep in the refrigerator for a week.

Grilled Romaine Salad with Steak and Sliced Tomatoes

30 MINUTES · *serves 4 to 6*

2 ears corn, shucked

1 head romaine lettuce, halved vertically (core intact)

Olive oil, for drizzling

Salt, to taste

1 avocado, pitted and cut into ½-inch pieces

½ cup **HONEY-LIME DRESSING**

12 to 16 ounces thinly sliced **GRILLED FLANK STEAK**

2 ounces sheep's milk feta cheese, crumbled

2 to 3 ripe tomatoes

1 **Grill the corn.** Light a grill to medium-high heat and grill the corn until fragrant and slightly charred. When it's cool enough to handle, cut the kernels off the cob into a medium bowl.

2 **Grill the romaine.** Rub the cut side of the romaine with a drizzle of oil and a pinch of salt. Place the romaine cut-side down and grill for 1 to 2 minutes. Turn and cook for another 1 to 2 minutes. Remove and discard the core, roughly chop, and transfer to a platter.

3 **Assemble the salad.** Combine the corn kernels and avocado. Drizzle in 2 tablespoons of the dressing and a pinch of salt. Stir to combine. Top lettuce with sliced steak and corn and avocado mixture. Drizzle more dressing over the salad and sprinkle with feta.

4 **Serve.** Slice tomatoes, sprinkle with salt, and serve alongside.

Grilled Vegetable Panini

15 MINUTES · *serves 4*

WHEN LITTLE LEAGUE PRACTICE is at 6:30 p.m. and you have to sit in traffic for 20 minutes to get there, sandwiches are the solution (and PB&J is solidly in that category). Here's a panini that helps things feel a little more like dinner, but with the convenience of your usual sandwich suspects.

It's super fast—you've already grilled the vegetables so it's mostly an assembly job. It's customizable—kids can take or leave the eggplant or basil; bonus if there are other odds and ends in the fridge that might taste good in a pressed sandwich. I like the gooey-briny combination of mozzarella and feta, but any melty cheese will work. I sometimes serve these with corn on the cob, but a quick cucumber salad (like the one on pg. 273) is also a good bet this time of year.

4 ciabatta rolls

½ cup **RED PEPPER-WALNUT SAUCE**

1 **GRILLED EGGPLANT**, sliced

2 **GRILLED ZUCCHINI**, sliced

1 large tomato, cored and cut into ¼-inch slices

8 to 10 basil leaves

4 to 6 ounces fresh mozzarella, torn into small pieces

2 ounces sheep's milk feta

Salt, to taste

Olive oil, for brushing the sandwiches

1 **Assemble the sandwiches**. Heat a large skillet or griddle over medium heat. Split the rolls and spread each side with the red pepper-walnut sauce. Add a layer of eggplant, zucchini, tomato, basil if using, and mozzarella and feta. Sprinkle with salt.

2 **Press.** Close the sandwiches, brush both sides with oil, and grill, pressing down with a spatula or another skillet, about 5 minutes on each side.

3 **Serve hot.** Or wrap in foil and take to go.

Cold Soba Noodle Salad

30 MINUTES · *serves 4 to 6*

WHAT IS IT ABOUT SOBA NOODLES on a hot summer night? When they're chilled and slippery and dressed up with some bright flavors, there's really nothing else I'd rather eat.

¼ cup rice vinegar

1 teaspoon salt

1 tablespoon granulated sugar

2 nectarines, pitted and cut into
  ¼-inch slices

½ small red onion, thinly sliced

1 pound **SOBA NOODLES**

½ teaspoon sesame oil

½ head napa cabbage, thinly sliced

¼ cup roughly chopped cilantro leaves

¼ cup roughly chopped mint leaves

¼ cup sesame seeds

1 **Quick pickle the nectarines and onions.** Whisk the vinegar, salt, and sugar together in a small bowl until the sugar dissolves. Add the nectarines and onions and set aside for 15 to 20 minutes.

2 **Cook the noodles according to package directions.** Drain, rinse, and blot dry with a paper towel. Toss with sesame oil and refrigerate until ready to use. (You can do this step in advance.)

3 **Assemble and serve.** In a large serving bowl, toss the noodles with the nectarines, onions, and vinegar mixture. Add the cabbage, cilantro, mint, and sesame seeds and toss well to combine.

Zucchini Fritters

45 MINUTES · *serves 4 to 6*

AS ANYONE WHO'S EVER GROWN ZUCCHINI or been part of a CSA knows, you can never have enough zucchini recipes—especially during that last gasp of warm weather. Fritters are a fantastic way to take advantage of an overabundance of vegetables, as is pizza (pg. 217), a frittata (pg. 85), or grain bowls (pg. 213).

Take a few minutes to throw together some Herby Yogurt Sauce (pg. 277); the tanginess sets off the rich fritters in the best way. Serve it all alongside the Simple Summer Salad (pg. 275) and a stack of warm pita.

2 small zucchini

¾ teaspoon salt, divided, plus more to taste

½ cup all-purpose flour

1 teaspoon baking soda

1 egg, lightly beaten

½ cup ricotta cheese

2 tablespoons chopped mint

Canola oil, for frying

TO SERVE

Pita bread

½ cup Herby Yogurt Sauce (pg. 277)

Simple Summer Salad (pg. 275)

1 **Make the batter.** Heat the oven to 250°F and set a cooling rack lined with paper towels on a rimmed baking sheet. Shred the zucchini into a medium bowl and toss with ½ teaspoon salt. Set aside. Whisk the flour, baking soda, and remaining salt together in a medium bowl. Add the egg and ricotta and mix well.

2 **Squeeze hard!** Transfer the zucchini to a colander and squeeze the liquid out of the zucchini. Line a sheet pan with paper towels and spread out the zucchini. Place paper towels on top and press to absorb any additional liquid. Discard the paper towels, gather up the zucchini, and stir it into the batter. Stir in the mint. Taste the batter and add more salt if needed.

3 **Fry.** Add enough canola oil to a large skillet over medium heat so it's about ¼-inch deep. When the oil shimmers, drop big spoonfuls of the batter into the pan. Cook for about 3 to 4 minutes, flip, and cook until the fritters are golden brown, another 3 to 4 minutes.

4 **Keep them warm.** Transfer to a cooling rack set on top of a baking sheet. Sprinkle with salt and let drain. Keep fritters and pita warm in the oven while you make a salad.

5 **Serve.** Place fritters on a platter and serve with warm pitas, yogurt sauce, and the salad.

LUNCHBOX GOALS

WHEN AUGUST ROLLS AROUND, I try my hardest not to think about the fall too much. The boys need new shoes and longer pants, but it's eighty degrees and I can't bear to shop for school supplies when the beach is a viable destination. But then something happens (it's called Labor Day) and I make lunchbox goals.

When Quincy first started kindergarten, I packed skewered olives, cheese, salami, tomatoes, and cucumbers. Some grapes and pita. They were beautiful lunches, but each day everything returned home in the lunchbox, warm and beat up, except for the grapes and pita. I made a quick return to sunbutter sandwiches, fruit, and yogurt for lunch, and focused my energy on dinner.

But the one lunchbox goal that has staying power is the occasional cookie that gets tucked in there. When I get in the groove, I bake up a batch then freeze the cookies (which thaw before lunch), or I keep a stash of dough in the fridge and bake small batches throughout the week. It feels special to pull fresh cookies out of the oven on a Wednesday night, and if you have dough on hand, the effort is minimal. And it makes my house smell good.

I'm always on the lookout for cookie recipes that fill the lunchbox criteria.

....

THEY SHOULD BE:

1. made from pantry ingredients

2. nut-free for school

3. not overloaded with crazy amounts of sugar

4. easy to work with and don't need to be chilled before baking (in case an eleventh hour urge to bake strikes)

....

One favorite came about by way of the five-pound bag of buckwheat flour I bought last year to play with. I was familiar with buckwheat from soba noodles and pancakes, but I'd never tried using it for baked goods. The flour is a little earthy and has a bitter edge that chocolate enhances in a really intriguing way. This cookie is not too sweet, which I like, and the boys don't notice because the chocolate flavor is so deep.

Chocolate-Buckwheat Cookies

30 MINUTES · *makes 24 cookies*

1 cup buckwheat flour

1 cup all-purpose flour

½ cup cocoa powder

½ teaspoon baking soda

½ teaspoon salt

2 sticks unsalted butter, melted

1 cup dark brown sugar

1 egg

1 teaspoon vanilla extract

6 ounces dark chocolate chunks

1 **Make the dough.** Heat the oven to 375°F and line 2 baking sheets with parchment paper. In a medium bowl, whisk together both flours, cocoa powder, baking soda, and salt and set aside. In a small bowl, mix together the melted butter, brown sugar, egg, and vanilla extract. Stir the wet ingredients into the dry mixture and combine thoroughly. Fold in the chocolate chunks.

2 **Bake.** Drop rounded tablespoons of dough onto the baking sheets about 2 inches apart. Bake, one sheet at a time, for about 10 minutes. Cool for at least 10 minutes before serving.

Early October

NORTHERN VEGETARIAN CHILI

BULGUR BOWLS WITH SWISS CHARD
AND ROASTED VEGETABLES

CORNMEAL CHEDDAR PANCAKES WITH PINTO BEANS

KALE PESTO PASTA

PIZZA NIGHT

APPLESAUCE CAKE

FALL IN NEW ENGLAND. It's pretty familiar, right? Pumpkin patches, hard-crunching apples, dreamy foliage, and the return of wooly scarves. All fabulous! But there are other elements in this shift from summer to fall: the weather, the light, and all that local produce changes drastically over these three months.

At this time of year, I'm most enamored of peppers in every shape, color, and heat level. They mature late in the summer, so when it's still warm enough to light the grill and eat outside, we grill bell peppers until their sweetness intensifies and they turn soft and smoky. I reach for them on the first or second soup night of the season to form the backbone of a hearty but light vegetarian chili. We also pickle, stuff, roast, purée, freeze, and eat them raw three times a day until one day, they disappear from the market. This menu makes sure we get our fill.

COME OCTOBER, I start itching to get back into the kitchen. So there's a fair amount of cooking happening this week, but most of it is pretty hands-off. And soon enough, a bowl of chili will be yours.

In the fall we return to cooking beans from dry. Don't forget to soak the pinto beans the night before. (I often put a reminder on my phone for this; without it, I forget and then the plan goes awry.) The next morning, get the beans on the stove and stick a pan of carrots and peppers in the oven to roast. This week's menu calls for roasted peppers and/or carrots in almost everything: grain bowls, salsa, and on top of pizza.

While the beans are cooking, prep the spices and vegetables for the chili. Make a batch of kale pesto, and if you have the time, wash, dry, and chop vegetables for salads. Toss together the dry ingredients for the pancakes if you really want to double down on advance prep.

THE BIG COOK

SOAK AND COOK THE PINTO BEANS

MAKE THE CHILI

ROAST 6 TO 8 RED PEPPERS AND
12 CARROTS FOR THE WEEK

COOK THE BULGUR

MAKE THE KALE PESTO

OTHER WAYS TO GET AHEAD

MAKE THE ROASTED RED PEPPER
SALSA (PG. 277)

WASH, DRY, AND CHOP THE SWISS CHARD

MIX THE DRY INGREDIENTS FOR PANCAKES

MAKE PIZZA DOUGH

Chili Traditions

I'M A FRENCH-IRISH MUTT from New England, so I have the fortune of being tethered to exactly zero chili traditions. I make what I like. I've stewed corn and squash with ground turkey and called it chili. I've made versions that are all about beans, others that are all about meat, and, via my husband Galen, I've learned to appreciate that weird concoction known as a Cincinnati Chili 5-Way. I also have a major crush on peppers in all forms, so even though this dish is vegetarian, the sweet and smoky flavors give it heft. Save leftovers for lunch tomorrow or freeze the rest to spice up a future dinner.

PINTO BEANS   MAKE AHEAD!

10 MINUTES ACTIVE, 2 HOURS TOTAL (AND AN OVERNIGHT SOAK) · *makes about 6 cups*

ANY TYPE OF DRIED CHILE will do here, but I particularly like anchos and anaheims for their mild spice. Once the beans are cooked, reserve 4 cups for the chili and the cornmeal pancakes. Freeze the remaining beans in their cooking liquid for later use.

1 pound dried pinto beans

1 teaspoon salt, plus more
  to taste

2 garlic cloves, lightly
  crushed

1 dried chile

1 bay leaf

1 **Soak the beans.** Put the beans in a bowl and cover with water. Soak overnight.

2 **Cook the beans.** Drain and rinse the beans and put them in a large pot with a lid (I use my 3-quart dutch oven). Cover with water by an inch, add the salt, and bring to a boil. Reduce to a simmer and add the garlic, chile, and bay leaf. Simmer for about 2 hours, until the beans are tender. Taste the broth and add more salt as needed.

Northern Vegetarian Chili

30 MINUTES ACTIVE, 2½ HOURS TOTAL · *serves 6 to 8*

2 teaspoons ground cumin

2 teaspoons dried ancho
chile powder

1 teaspoon smoked paprika

1 teaspoon cocoa powder

½ teaspoon ground cinnamon

1 teaspoon salt, plus more to taste

2 tablespoons canola oil

2 medium yellow onions, chopped

2 tablespoons tomato paste

4 garlic cloves, chopped

4 to 6 sweet peppers, chopped

28-ounce can crushed tomatoes

8 cups vegetable stock or water

2 dried chiles

1 bay leaf

1 sprig sage (3 to 4 leaves, plus
the stem)

½ cinnamon stick

3 cups **COOKED PINTO BEANS**

Freshly ground black pepper,
to taste

GARNISHES

½ cup plain yogurt

Chopped cilantro

1 to 2 scallions, green parts only,
or ¼ white onion, chopped

1 **Prepare spices.** In a small bowl, mix together the cumin, chile powder, paprika, cocoa powder, ground cinnamon, and salt. Set aside.

2 **Sauté onions.** Set a large, heavy-bottomed pot over medium heat. Warm the oil, then add the onions and cook, stirring, for 2 to 3 minutes. Add the tomato paste and half of the spice mixture. Continue to cook, stirring, until the ingredients are combined and the onions have softened, about 3 minutes. Add the garlic and cook, stirring, for another 2 to 3 minutes.

3 **Add the peppers.** Combine them with the onions and spices and cook for 20 to 25 minutes, stirring from time to time. Don't rush this step—the peppers develop great flavor as they release their water and soften. Stir in the tomatoes, add the water or stock and another pinch of salt, increase the heat to medium-high, and bring to a boil.

4 **Simmer.** Reduce heat to medium-low and add the dried chiles, bay leaf, sage, and cinnamon stick. Simmer, uncovered, for 60 to 70 minutes, stirring occasionally. Stir in the cooked pinto beans and the remaining spice mix and continue simmering for another 20 to 30 minutes.

5 **Taste.** Adjust seasoning and discard dried chiles, bay leaf, cinnamon stick, and sage leaves.

6 **Serve.** Set out chili and garnishes.

Roasted + Ready

WHEN I LOOK AT THE WEEK AHEAD and see an extra crazy night on the horizon, I plan for a meal just like this. If all goes according to plan, roasted peppers and carrots will be waiting for me in the fridge, alongside prepped bulgur (maybe I even made a double batch so I could use some for lunch salads). All I need to do is sauté the chard, fry up a few eggs, and toss it all into bowls with a bit of freshly torn mint, salt, and pepper. Dinner, done—sanity, intact.

ROASTED PEPPERS AND CARROTS

MAKE AHEAD!

Peppers can be grilled (pg. 272) or broiled (it's quicker)—but if you're roasting other vegetables, you can knock both out at once. For this meal, simply put them in the 450°F oven first, as they'll take about 10 minutes longer than the carrots (30 to 40 minutes total).

For the carrots, I like to find smallish ones and roast them whole. If I can't find those, I cut large carrots in half vertically, which makes for a pretty presentation. Toss them with olive oil, sprinkle with salt, and roast until tender, 20 to 25 minutes.

BULGUR

1 cup dry bulgur

2 cups water or stock

Juice and zest of 1 lemon

¼ cup chopped parsley

½ teaspoon cinnamon

½ teaspoon allspice

½ teaspoon sumac (optional)

Salt, to taste

Freshly ground black pepper, to taste

Place the bulgur in a medium bowl. Bring the water or stock to a boil and pour over the bulgur. Cover and let sit for about 30 minutes. Strain through a sieve, pressing out any liquid. Stir in the lemon juice and zest, parsley, and spices, and season to taste.

Bulgur Bowls with Swiss Chard and Roasted Vegetables

30 MINUTES ACTIVE, 45 MINUTES TOTAL • *serves 4*

1 bunch swiss chard

1 tablespoon olive oil

½ medium yellow onion, chopped

Salt, to taste

2 garlic cloves, minced

Splash of red wine vinegar

3 **ROASTED CARROTS**, roughly chopped

2 **ROASTED BELL PEPPERS**, roughly chopped

4 eggs

Olive oil, for frying eggs

2 cups **COOKED BULGUR**

4 ounces sheep's milk feta, crumbled

2 tablespoons torn mint leaves

Pinch of red pepper flakes, optional

1 **Prep the chard.** Separate the chard stems from the leaves. Chop the stems into ¼-inch pieces and roughly chop the leaves into 1- or 2-inch pieces.

2 **Sauté.** Place a large pan over medium heat and add the oil. When it shimmers, add the chard stems, onions, and a pinch of salt and cook, stirring, until the vegetables start to soften, about 5 minutes. Add the garlic and continue to cook for another 2 to 3 minutes. Add the chard leaves and continue to cook, stirring, until they wilt completely and are coated in the oil, 5 to 7 minutes. Stir in the vinegar; season to taste.

3 **Finish and serve.** Add the carrots and peppers to the skillet to warm through. In another skillet, fry the eggs. Divide bulgur into 4 bowls, then top with vegetables. Add a fried egg to each and top with crumbled feta and mint leaves. Add red pepper flakes if desired.

Cornmeal Cheddar Pancakes with Pinto Beans

30 MINUTES · *serves 4 to 6*

PANCAKES REMIND ME OF MY DAD, whose cooking repertoire was basically nonexistent, except for breakfast foods like bacon, eggs, and pancakes. I doubt he ever would have made this savory cornmeal version studded with melted cheese, but as a champion of the breakfast-for-dinner philosophy, he would have enjoyed eating them. I like to serve these for dinner topped with pinto beans, Roasted Red Pepper Salsa (pg. 277), chopped scallions, and cilantro. If you have leftovers, heat them in a skillet for breakfast the next morning—this time with a dad-approved setup of fruit and maple syrup.

1 cup **PINTO BEANS**

1¼ cups cornmeal

¾ cup all-purpose flour

2 teaspoons baking powder

¼ teaspoon baking soda

¼ teaspoon salt

2 tablespoons honey

2 eggs

1¼ cups buttermilk (or 1 cup plain yogurt, thinned with milk or water)

2 tablespoons unsalted butter, melted and cooled

4 ounces cheddar cheese, cut into ¼-inch cubes

Canola oil, for frying

TO SERVE

ROASTED RED PEPPER SALSA (pg. 277) (or store-bought)

½ cup plain yogurt

2 to 3 scallions, green parts only, chopped

Chopped cilantro

1 **Warm the beans.** Put the beans in a small saucepan and keep on the back burner over low heat. Heat the oven to 200°F and have a rimmed baking sheet on hand.

2 **Mix the dry ingredients.** In a large bowl, mix together the cornmeal, flour, baking powder, baking soda, and salt.

3 **Add the wet ingredients.** In a medium bowl, whisk together the honey, eggs, buttermilk, and butter. Combine this mixture with the dry ingredients (taking care not to over mix). Fold in the cheddar.

4 **Make the pancakes.** Heat a large skillet or griddle over medium heat for about 5 minutes. Add just enough oil to thinly coat the pan. When the oil is warm, pour the batter onto the griddle— about ¼ cup for each pancake. Cook until the batter bubbles and the pancakes brown at the edges, 3 to 4 minutes. Flip and cook for another 3 to 4 minutes. Transfer the pancakes to the baking sheet, place in the oven to keep warm, and repeat with remaining batter.

5 **Serve.** Set out the pancakes with pinto beans and salsa. Garnish with plain yogurt, scallions, and chopped cilantro.

The Power of Pesto

KALE IS A STAPLE IN MY DIET, but the boys are still skeptical. This rich and nutty pesto nudges them toward acceptance—and it pleases me because I can make a batch, freeze it in an ice cube tray, and grab cubes when I need them, making a dinner like this incredibly easy. If your eating companions require a bit more, toss in some white beans or serve alongside sausages. For a simple side dish, warm the leftover roasted carrots in a skillet with a little olive oil and shower with lemon juice, chopped mint, and parsley, or try the Roasted Red Peppers and Carrots with Feta (pg. 272).

KALE PESTO   MAKE AHEAD!

10 MINUTES · *makes 1½ cups*

1 bunch lacinato kale, stemmed and torn into 1-inch pieces

1 garlic clove, peeled and roughly chopped

½ cup toasted walnuts, skins rubbed off and roughly chopped

½ cup olive oil

¼ cup finely grated parmesan

1 to 2 tablespoons lemon juice

1 teaspoon lemon zest

½ teaspoon salt, plus more to taste

Place the kale in the bowl of a food processor fitted with the steel chopping blade and chop until coarse. Add the garlic and walnuts and pulse to combine. When it forms a chunky paste, slowly add the olive oil (with the motor running). Transfer to a bowl and stir in the cheese, lemon juice and zest, and salt. Taste and adjust seasoning.

Kale Pesto Pasta

20 MINUTES · *serves 4 to 6*

1 pound penne, or similarly shaped pasta

¾ cup **KALE PESTO**

1 ounce shaved parmesan, for garnish

1 **Make pasta.** Cook pasta according to package directions, reserving ½ cup pasta water. Drain the pasta and return to the saucepan over medium-low heat.

2 **Add pesto.** Add a splash of pasta water and the pesto. Stir to warm the pesto and coat the pasta, adding more pasta water as needed to make a silky sauce. Taste and adjust seasoning.

3 **Serve.** Divide between shallow bowls and garnish with shaved parmesan.

Pizza Night

20 MINUTES ACTIVE, 30 MINUTES TOTAL · *serves 4*

ON FRIDAYS, THE PULL OF TAKEOUT is strong. But stretching dough, shredding cheese, and picking out toppings is much more fun. So on the tired nights when I can remember that fact (along with the reality that two homemade pizzas cost less than half of one takeout pie), we get down to business and let takeout take the win another time.

Cornmeal

1 ball of pizza dough, store-bought or homemade (pg. 281)

Olive oil

½ cup ricotta

¼ cup **KALE PESTO**

2 **ROASTED RED BELL PEPPERS,** roughly chopped

2 ounces fresh mozzarella, torn into small pieces

1 to 2 ounces parmesan, finely grated

¼ cup packed basil leaves

Salt, to taste

Freshly ground black pepper, to taste

1 **Get ready.** Heat the oven to 500°F. Position a rack in the bottom third of the oven. Sprinkle a rimmed sheet pan with cornmeal.

2 **Make the pizza.** Stretch the dough to fit the sheet pan and brush with olive oil. Spread with ricotta, then scatter small spoonfuls of pesto on top. Add the chopped peppers, followed by the mozzarella and parmesan.

3 **Finish and serve.** Bake until the dough browns and the cheese bubbles, 10 to 12 minutes. Transfer pizza to a cutting board and let it rest. Sprinkle with basil leaves and season to taste.

On the Cusp

MY YOUNGER SON ELLIS'S BIRTHDAY falls in the third week of October—the cusp of mid-to-late fall, the cusp of Libra-to-Scorpio. His birthday could be a sun-warmed, bright, clear day, or a blustery gray one. When he turned three, we decided that, rather than invite ten three-year-olds and their parents and siblings to come eat cake and bounce off the walls of our little condo, we'd move operations to the closest playground. No walls and minimal mess. Wins all around.

Living in the little place we do, we're used to packing up a party and bringing it somewhere else—to the park, to my mom's house, on our old boat, to a campsite. For the playground party, I planned no-harm, no-foul food that would be fine sitting out on a windy playground for a couple of hours: bagels and cream cheese, a fancy cheese plate for the grownups, grapes and clementines, and an applesauce cake served with clouds of whipped cream (ok, this one took a little extra TLC, but it was a birthday party after all). One thermos of hot coffee and another of hot mulled cider. Plenty of cups, plus bags for the trash.

I'm not sure how many more years I'll get to make this homey little cake for Ellis's birthday before he starts asking for a Ninja Turtle-shaped cake frosted with three inches of bright green icing, but I'm going to run with it while I can. Applesauce—especially the kind we make from apples we picked—still delights both boys to the extent that applesauce cake is just an over-the-top exciting idea.

Applesauce Cake

30 MINUTES ACTIVE, 2 HOURS TOTAL · *serves 12*

2 cups all-purpose flour

2 teaspoons baking powder

½ teaspoon baking soda

½ teaspoon salt

½ teaspoon cinnamon

½ teaspoon nutmeg

½ teaspoon ground cardamom

½ teaspoon ground allspice

10 tablespoons unsalted butter
(1 stick plus 2 tablespoons), room
temperature

1 cup granulated sugar

½ cup packed dark brown sugar

2 large eggs

1 teaspoon vanilla extract

1¼ cups unsweetened applesauce

GLAZE

1 cup confectioner's sugar, sifted

3 tablespoons apple cider

Squirt lemon juice

1 **Get ready.** Heat the oven to 350°F. Butter a 12-cup Bundt pan, then dust the inside with flour. Whisk together the flour, baking powder, baking soda, salt, and spices in a medium bowl.

2 **Make the batter.** In a stand mixer fitted with the paddle attachment, cream together the butter and both sugars on medium speed until light and fluffy, about 5 minutes. Add 1 egg at a time, scraping down the sides of the bowl and beating until the eggs are fully combined. Add the vanilla extract and beat to combine. Add the dry mixture, one third at a time, scraping down the sides of the bowl and beating until the ingredients are fully incorporated each time. Add the applesauce and beat on low until just combined, less than a minute.

3 **Bake.** Pour the cake batter into the prepared Bundt pan. Place on the middle rack of the oven. Bake until a skewer inserted into the center of the cake comes out clean, 45 to 50 minutes. Cool the cake in the pan for about 15 minutes before inverting it onto a cooling rack. Cool completely before glazing.

4 **Make the glaze.** Place sugar in a small bowl and whisk in cider (1 tablespoon at a time) and lemon juice, until glaze is thick but pourable. Set aside.

5 **Glaze the cake.** Place the cake on the cooling rack over a sheet pan and drizzle the glaze over the top. Give the glaze about 30 minutes to set. Serve with whipped cream on the side.

Late October

TACOS • SIMPLE SLAW

CURRIED BUTTERNUT SQUASH SOUP •
APPLE & WALNUT SALAD

SCHMANCY GRILLED CHEESE • BEET SALAD
WITH GRAIN MUSTARD VINAIGRETTE

TAMARIND CHICKPEAS OVER RICE

FRIDAY NIGHT CHICKEN POT PIE

ROBESON RYE

BY LATE OCTOBER, warm-weather crops are officially finished. Goodbye, peppers and corn. Hello, acorn and butternut and delicata and kuri: I shall roast you, stuff you, make you into soup (mwa hah hah!).

At this time of year, I definitely feel a shift in tempo. Summer is well in the rear view, and the holidays aren't right on top of us yet, so our weekly routines have a better chance of running smoothly. We're having neighborhood friends for dinner more often and hitting our Saturday market for big bags of apples, stalks of brussels sprouts, and our weekly bagel fix. Shorter, blustery days mean more time spent puttering in the kitchen, happily prepping for the week ahead.

Dinner

week of 10/17

Mon TACOS

Tue butternut soup
apple walnut
salad

Wed grilled cheese
beet salad

Thu tamarind
chickpeas +
rice

Fri chicken pot pie

IT'S ALSO AROUND THIS TIME OF YEAR when the whole poached chicken goes into heavy rotation in my kitchen. Submerging a whole bird in water and simmering with aromatics is strategic: The hands-off process gives you both meat and stock, which anchor three of the week's meals and then some. While the bird is cooking, batch roast the squash and beets and go for a walk. When you come back, half of the week's prep will be done.

THE BIG COOK

POACH A CHICKEN AND MAKE
THE STOCK

ROAST THE BEETS (PG. 272)

ROAST THE BUTTERNUT SQUASH

MAKE THE GRAIN MUSTARD
VINAIGRETTE (PG. 276)

OTHER WAYS TO GET AHEAD

TOAST WALNUTS FOR THE SALAD

SOAK AND COOK THE CHICKPEAS;
CHOP THE CAULIFLOWER FOR THE
TAMARIND CHICKPEAS

The Utility Player

I ADORE THIS METHOD FOR MAKING STOCK and cooking a bird at the same time, which I learned from chef Andrea Reusing's 2011 book, *Cooking in the Moment*. The meat is never overcooked and the stock is super flavorful. Whenever I use this method, I have a plan in mind for the chicken meat and the stock that week. Usually it's tacos one night and chicken pot pie later in the week (that's the game plan here). After I make some soup, I freeze whatever stock remains. If I'm swimming in it, I'll use chicken stock to cook pasta or rice, or splash it into beans or greens I'm heating up.

STOCK PLUS

15 MINUTES ACTIVE, 1½ TO 2 HOURS TOTAL · *makes about 10 cups stock, plus 3 to 4 cups shredded chicken meat*

---

1 3 to 4 pound chicken, rinsed and patted dry, gizzard and liver removed

1 tablespoon salt

1 medium yellow onion, peeled and quartered

3 celery sticks, halved

2 carrots, halved

2 leeks, halved lengthwise

1 to 2 bay leaves

8 to 10 peppercorns

1 **Prep the chicken.** Liberally salt the chicken all over; don't be shy. Put it in a large stockpot and cover by an inch with cold water. Add the remaining ingredients and bring to a boil over high heat.

2 **Poach.** Once boiling, reduce the heat to a simmer and cook for 5 minutes. Turn off the heat and cover the pot. After an hour, the chicken will be perfectly cooked but still too hot to handle. Remove the lid and let it cool for a while in the pot (30 minutes or so).

3 **Remove the meat.** Once cooled, pull the chicken from the pot, pick all of the meat off of it, and store the meat, covered, in the refrigerator. It will keep in the refrigerator for about 5 days.

4 **Continue making the stock.** Return the chicken carcass to the pot, bring to a simmer over medium-high heat, and simmer for 1 hour, skimming any foam that rises to the top.

5 **Finish and store.** Strain the stock, removing bones and aromatics. Taste and adjust seasoning. Let the stock cool, skim the fat off of the top, then pour it into Mason jars or freezer bags for storage. Stock will keep in the refrigerator for about 1 week and in the freezer for months, but I like to use it within 1 to 2 months.

Tacos · Simple Slaw

45 MINUTES · *serves 4*

THIS IS ONE OF OUR TIME-TESTED DINNERS—popular because (you guessed it!) everyone makes his or her own. One child might just want plain yogurt on his tortilla (ugh, fine) and the other will need to have the avocado pried out of his hand. I like taco night best when there are bowls upon bowls of potential toppings—from inky, saucy black beans to pickled jalapeños and a couple of different salsas and shredded or roasted vegetables. It puts less pressure on the chicken to be the main event, and the variety is part of the fun.

¼ head red cabbage, cored and thinly shredded

½ teaspoon salt, plus more to taste

1½ cups **PULLED CHICKEN**

¾ cup salsa verde, divided

15-ounce can black beans, drained

½ cup corn kernels, thawed if frozen

12 corn tortillas

1 lime, divided

¼ cup chopped cilantro

GARNISHES

1 lime, cut into wedges

1 avocado, pitted and cubed

PICKLED JALAPEÑOS (pg. 270)

Plain yogurt

Shredded cheddar or jack cheese

Chopped cilantro

1 **Start the slaw.** In a medium bowl, rub the cabbage with the salt and set aside.

2 **Warm the chicken and beans.** Put the pulled chicken and ½ cup salsa verde in a small saucepan over low heat. Put ¼ cup salsa verde in another small saucepan with the beans and corn. Stir to combine, add a pinch of salt, and set over low heat.

3 **Prepare the tortillas.** Gently warm 12 tortillas, transfer to a plate, and cover with a towel.

4 **Finish the slaw.** Drain the cabbage, return it to the bowl, and toss with the juice of half a lime.

5 **Serve.** Transfer the slaw, chicken, and beans to serving bowls. Sprinkle the beans with the juice of half a lime and some cilantro. Place the lime wedges, avocado, jalapeños, yogurt, cheese, and chopped cilantro in small bowls. Serve with tortillas.

Soup to Nuts

BUTTERNUT SQUASH SOUP IS A FLEXIBLE TEMPLATE for whatever spices, aromatics, and garnishes strike you. On chilly fall nights, it's especially nice curried, with a mix of freshly toasted and ground spices, and served alongside a salad with a lot of crunch and traditional autumn flavors.

I usually mix up my own version of garam masala: Combine ½ teaspoon each cumin seeds, coriander seeds, cloves, cardamom pods, and black peppercorns. Toast and grind in a spice grinder, mix with ½ teaspoon ground cinnamon. You'll have more than you need but it will keep. (Use it again for the tamarind chickpeas!)

A simple soup like this is a perfect vehicle for homemade chicken stock, and that's where the planning piece of batch cooking comes into play. If I'm making soup and pot pie, I make sure I have enough stock to go around. But if I run short, I'd prioritize the pot pie (to amplify the chicken flavor) and fill in any gaps with water—between the assertive spices and the sweet, roasted squash, you'll hardly notice the difference.

An immersion blender streamlines things, but if you don't have one, buzz the soup in batches in a regular blender. And this soup is a solid candidate to double and freeze half the batch. It will keep in the refrigerator for four to five days and in the freezer for two months.

ROASTED BUTTERNUT SQUASH   MAKE AHEAD!

10 MINUTES ACTIVE, 1 HOUR TOTAL

ROASTING THE SQUASH INTENSIFIES THE FLAVOR and is a hands-off way to cut down on the time it takes to make the soup. Get this done a few days ahead and you'll have dinner on the table in no time. The roasted squash will keep in the refrigerator for 4 to 5 days.

2 medium butternut squash, halved vertically and seeded

1 tablespoon olive oil

1 teaspoon salt

Heat the oven to 375°F and rub the squash all over with oil and salt. Place the squash cut-side down on a rimmed baking sheet and roast until it is cooked through, 45 to 50 minutes. Set aside to cool, then remove and discard the skin.

Curried Butternut Squash Soup · Apple & Walnut Salad

30 MINUTES ACTIVE, 1 HOUR TOTAL · *serves 4 (with leftovers for the freezer)*

1 tablespoon olive oil

1 medium yellow onion, chopped

1 teaspoon salt, plus more to taste

2-inch piece ginger, peeled and finely grated

2 teaspoons ground turmeric

2½ teaspoons garam masala, divided

2 medium **BUTTERNUT SQUASH**, roasted

10 cups **CHICKEN STOCK**, water, or a combination of both

TO SERVE

1 lime, quartered

¼ cup coconut flakes

¼ cup pumpkin seeds

2 tablespoons chopped cilantro

APPLE & WALNUT SALAD

4 to 6 cups mixed greens

2 tablespoons olive oil

½ cup parsley leaves

½ cup toasted walnuts, skins rubbed off and roughly chopped

1 apple, cut into matchsticks

Splash of sherry vinegar

Salt, to taste

Freshly ground black pepper, to taste

1 **Make the soup.** In a large, heavy-bottomed pot, heat the oil over medium heat. When the oil shimmers, add the onion and cook until translucent, about 5 minutes. Add a pinch of salt along with the ginger and cook for 2 more minutes. Add the turmeric and 1½ teaspoons of the garam masala and cook, stirring, for an additional 3 minutes.

2 **Add the roasted squash.** Stir to combine with the onion and spices. Add the stock and/or water and stir to combine. Bring to a boil, reduce heat to a simmer, add the teaspoon of salt, and cook for about 30 minutes.

3 **Purée.** Using an immersion blender, buzz until smooth. Add the remaining teaspoon of garam masala. Simmer over low heat for 10 more minutes, adjust seasoning to taste.

4 **Toast the coconut.** While the soup is simmering, place the coconut in a dry skillet over medium-low heat and cook, stirring, until toasted, 3 to 5 minutes. Set aside.

5 **Make the salad.** Place the greens in a salad bowl and toss with olive oil. Add the parsley, walnuts, and apples and toss to combine. Add the vinegar, toss, add salt to taste, and toss once more. Finish with a grind of black pepper.

6 **Serve.** Ladle the soup into bowls and garnish with a squeeze of lime juice and a sprinkle of toasted coconut, pumpkin seeds, and cilantro. Serve alongside the salad.

Schmancy Grilled Cheese ·
Beet Salad with Grain Mustard Vinaigrette

20 MINUTES ACTIVE, 30 MINUTES TOTAL · *serves 4*

WE HAVE SANDWICHES FOR DINNER at least once a week (and sometimes more). They have mass appeal and they can go in any direction you want. Take this fancy grilled cheese, which I make with dense country bread and a mix of cheeses. A swipe of honey gilds the lily and serving it alongside a roasted beet salad makes it downright elegant.

BEET SALAD WITH GRAIN MUSTARD VINAIGRETTE

2 to 3 **ROASTED BEETS** (pg. 272)

1 cup mixed greens

½ cup chopped parsley leaves, plus more for garnish

½ cup toasted walnuts, chopped

4 ounces goat cheese

Salt, to taste

Freshly ground black pepper, to taste

¼ cup **GRAIN MUSTARD VINAIGRETTE** (pg. 276)

GRILLED CHEESE

4 tablespoons unsalted butter, at room temperature

8 slices crusty bread

2 tablespoons honey—I like unfiltered raw honey; it's thicker and easy to spread

12 ounces cheddar or a mix of cheddar and Alpine cheese (Gruyere or Comte), shredded

1 **Make the beet salad.** Peel and cut roasted beets into 1-inch cubes. Toss the beets in a salad bowl with greens, parsley, and walnuts. Set aside.

2 **Make the grilled cheese.** Heat a large cast iron skillet or griddle over medium heat. Spread butter on 1 side of each slice of bread and a thin layer of honey on the other side. Divide the cheese between 4 slices of bread (buttered side out), top with the remaining slices, and place each sandwich on the skillet. Adjust heat to medium-low if the bread is browning faster than the cheese is melting. Cook until the cheese is completely melted and the bread is a toasty, golden brown, about 5 minutes on each side.

3 **Finish and serve.** Toss salad with vinaigrette and season with a pinch of salt and a grind of black pepper. Sprinkle with goat cheese and serve alongside grilled cheese

Tamarind Chickpeas over Rice

45 MINUTES · *serves 4 to 6*

THIS RECIPE IS INSPIRED BY Julie Sahni's 1980 cookbook *Classic Indian Cooking*. The technique for browning the onions uses more oil and heat than I'm accustomed to, but the resulting flavor is intensely rich and satisfying. Adding tamarind layers the dish with a lovely puckery-sour flavor.

⅓ cup vegetable oil

1 large yellow onion, thinly sliced

1 medium garlic clove, minced

1-inch piece ginger, shredded
   over the big holes of a box grater

½ teaspoon turmeric

½ teaspoon dried chile powder
   (optional)

1 cup crushed tomatoes in
   their juices

1 cup water or stock

½ head cauliflower, cut into ½-inch
   pieces

2 cups **CHICKPEAS**, cooked from dry
   (or use canned)

2 teaspoons garam masala (pg. 228)

1 tablespoon tamarind paste

1 teaspoon salt, plus more to taste

1 cup frozen green peas

TO SERVE

Basmati rice

½ cup whole milk yogurt

2 tablespoons chopped cilantro

1. **Cook the onions.** Heat the oil in a large, heavy pan (I use my dutch oven) over medium to medium-high heat. When the oil shimmers, add the onions and cook for 15 to 20 minutes, stirring frequently. After 7 to 10 minutes, they'll start to brown and clump together. Watch closely and keep stirring; turn down heat if they start to smoke or blacken. After 12 to 15 minutes, onions should be deep brown and a little shriveled, but not black or burnt.

2. **Sauté the aromatics.** Add the garlic, ginger, turmeric, and chile powder (if using) and cook for 2 more minutes. Add the tomatoes, then reduce heat to medium and cook, stirring, for another 5 minutes. At this point, the mixture should look like it's separating; that's what you want.

3. **Add the cauliflower.** Stir in the water and the cauliflower, then cover and simmer for about 15 minutes, until the cauliflower is tender. Add the chickpeas and the garam masala and simmer for another 7 to 10 minutes.

4. **Season the chickpeas.** (If you have tamarind-phobes at the table, ladle out their portions now.) Add the tamarind and stir to combine, season to taste. The dish may need to simmer for a few more minutes so the flavors bloom; use your judgment.

5. **Make the rice.** While the curry is simmering, cook the rice, 15 to 25 minutes (see pg. 280 for helpful hints).

6. **Finish and serve.** Add the peas during the last 2 to 3 minutes of cooking and stir to combine. Ladle the curry over rice, and garnish with dollops of yogurt and a sprinkle of chopped cilantro.

Carving Out Time

I LOVE THE PROCESS OF MAKING POT PIE—simmering the stock, making a roux, rolling pastry. It's a roll-up-your-sleeves project of the best kind. It can be tough to find a big enough chunk of time to make pot pie in one fell swoop, so sometimes I break it down into a series of steps I can take over the course of a few days. I make the stock and the chicken on a Sunday, then prep the vegetables and make the filling on a weeknight evening after the kids go to bed.

Weeknights are compressed and full of to-dos. But when I carve out an hour or so for a project like this, I find it restorative (I'll even go as far as scheduling it on the calendar). The kitchen is quiet and clean(ish), and I tune into the smell of stock simmering on the back burner, to the magical way a roux-thickened sauce comes together. The pleasure of cooking at times like these helps gird me for the next 6 p.m. dinner rush when water can't boil fast enough and people are melting down at the table because I served the wrong color cheese.

Once the filling is made, I refrigerate it in the same vessel in which I'll bake it. On pot pie night, all that's left to do is to roll out the dough, lay it over the filling, and put that bad boy in the oven for an hour.

I like to serve this on Friday nights. We get home earlier than usual, make popcorn, and start a movie while the pot pie bakes. Maybe I'll make the grownups a couple of well-deserved cocktails while we wait. When it's close to done, I toss mixed greens with vinaigrette. When the movie's over, we eat dinner. No sweat, no meltdowns.

Friday Night Chicken Pot Pie

1 HOUR ACTIVE, 2 HOURS TOTAL · *serves 6*

2 cups **CHICKEN STOCK**

½ cup whole milk

2 bay leaves

2 thyme sprigs

1 teaspoon salt, divided

3 tablespoons butter

1 large leek, thick green tops removed, halved vertically and cut into ½-inch slices

1 large carrot, peeled and cut into ½-inch dice

1 small fennel bulb, trimmed and cut into ½-inch dice

3 tablespoons all-purpose flour

½ teaspoon freshly ground black pepper, plus more to taste

¼ teaspoon freshly grated nutmeg

Tabasco sauce, to taste

2½ cups **PULLED CHICKEN**, cut or shredded into 1-inch pieces

1 cup frozen peas

¼ cup heavy cream

Juice of ½ lemon

2 tablespoons chopped parsley

1 egg, beaten

Half of a 14-ounce sheet of all-butter puff pastry (I like Dufour), thawed

1 **Warm the stock.** Combine the stock, milk, bay leaves, thyme, and a pinch of salt in a medium saucepan and bring to a simmer over medium heat. Simmer for 4 to 5 minutes, then reduce heat to medium-low and keep warm, stirring occasionally, until ready to use. Discard bay leaves and thyme before using.

2 **Cook the vegetables.** Melt the butter in a medium saucepan over medium heat. When it foams, add the leeks and a pinch of salt and cook, stirring, until they soften and wilt, 3 to 5 minutes. Add the carrots and fennel and a pinch of salt and cook, stirring, until the vegetables just soften, 5 to 7 minutes. Sprinkle the flour over the vegetables and cook, stirring, for 3 to 5 minutes.

3 **Add the stock.** Slowly whisk in the warm stock until the mixture is incorporated. Raise the heat just a nudge (not quite to medium-high) so the sauce starts bubbling slowly. Cook, stirring, for another 8 to 10 minutes to let the sauce thicken a bit.

4 **Season.** Lower the heat to medium and stir in the pepper, nutmeg, and a dash of Tabasco. Taste and adjust seasoning. Cook, stirring, for about 5 more minutes. Adjust the heat as needed, so that the sauce continues bubbling slowly and isn't sticking to the bottom of the pan.

5 **Finish the filling.** Turn off the heat and stir in the chicken, peas, cream, lemon juice, and parsley. Taste once more and adjust the seasoning as needed. Transfer the filling to a 9x11 inch baking dish and refrigerate for about 10 minutes. (Filling can be covered and refrigerated at this point for up to 3 days.)

6 **Assemble the pot pie.** Heat the oven to 400°F. Remove the baking dish from the refrigerator and brush the rim with egg wash.

7 **Get rolling.** Flour a work surface and unfold the half sheet of pastry over it. Roll out the dough into a 10x12 inch sheet. Lift the pastry and lay it over the top of the filling. Press the overhanging crust against the edges of the baking dish, crimping as needed. Brush the top of the pastry with the egg wash. Cut 2 to 3 vents in the pastry to allow steam to escape when baking.

8 **Bake.** Bake at 400°F for 15 minutes, then reduce heat to 375°F and bake until the filling bubbles up through the vents in the crust and the pastry is golden brown, another 40 to 45 minutes.

9 **Finish and serve.** Cool for 10 to 15 minutes before serving. Serve warm with a green salad alongside.

Robeson Rye

Makes 2 drinks

SINCE IT'S FRIDAY and there's not much work to do once the pot pie goes into the oven, you might as well have a cocktail while dinner bakes. Make sure there are snacks for the underage set, too, so no one implodes before dinner hits the table.

1 ounce Cardamaro

4 ounces rye whiskey

2 ounces maple syrup

Few dashes orange bitters

2 pieces of orange peel

Chill two cocktail glasses in the freezer for at least 20 minutes.

Divide the Cardamaro evenly between the 2 glasses and "wash" the glasses with it by tilting and swirling the glasses to coat them.

Fill a cocktail mixer halfway with ice and add the rye, maple syrup, and orange bitters. Stir gently until chilled and combined. Strain into glasses and rub the rim of each glass with an orange peel. Float the orange peel in the drink and serve.

November

BRAISED PORK SHOULDER OVER POLENTA

MARCELLA'S MEATBALLS WITH POLENTA SQUARES

PULLED PORK SANDWICHES • RED CABBAGE SLAW

BBQ WINGS • OVEN FRIES

SEARED SCALLOPS • FETTUCCINE WITH SPINACH & BACON

MAPLE-ALMOND GRANOLA

NOVEMBER IS AN AUSTERE MONTH. Gray skies, bare trees, rain that rushes you home. On rare sunny days, we seize the waning light and play outside until it's almost dark. Even then, it's only 5 p.m. The upside to the lack of daylight is that we're home earlier, with a little more breathing room before sitting down to dinner. The boys have a snack, get absorbed in an activity, I make dinner, and—on a good night—we sit down at six.

camanders
OffiCe.

Keep out.

For nieht
NINJa's only.

PORK SHOULDER STARS on the menu this week. Set it in the oven to braise, and you'll have the rest of your prep done and organized for the week by dinnertime. November can get busy, so this menu has a few dishes that can be doubled (or tripled) and stocked in the freezer for when the pace picks up at Thanksgiving.

Polenta is a workhorse ingredient that I love to have on hand this time of year. It's a winner served soft as a cushion for braised pork, but I also use it as a base for wilted greens and a fried egg. It firms up when refrigerated and can be pan-fried or brushed with a little olive oil and baked, making a sturdy and versatile base for just about any protein, vegetable, or even fruit. (Try it with sautéed apples and maple syrup.)

Later in the week, make the barbeque sauce and salt the chicken wings a day ahead of time—these little tasks can be easily done during dinner cleanup.

THE BIG COOK

PREP, SEASON, AND BRAISE THE PORK

MAKE THE MEATBALLS

COOK A DOUBLE BATCH OF POLENTA

OTHER WAYS TO GET AHEAD

SHRED CABBAGE FOR THE SLAW

PICKLE THE RED ONIONS (PG. 270)

SALT THE CHICKEN THE NIGHT BEFORE BAKING

MAKE THE BARBEQUE SAUCE

Pleasing the Crowd

BRAISED PORK IS A GREAT DISH to have in the repertoire—it's a crowd pleaser that's delightfully adaptable to different flavors. I love this particular flavor profile, but you could try any number of combinations: milk and fennel, apple cider with onions, or red wine and rosemary. Just play around with it and this dish will quickly become second nature. For the best flavor, season the pork the night before, but if you missed this step, don't fret—just do it at least thirty minutes ahead so the salt has some time to penetrate the meat.

Braising a pork shoulder takes some time, but it's mostly hands-off. This recipe produces enough pork for two meals in my house, but adjust the quantity of meat as you see fit.

BRAISED PORK SHOULDER

30 MINUTES ACTIVE, 3½ HOURS TOTAL · *serves 8 to 10*

2 teaspoons ground cumin

2 teaspoons dried chile powder (I use ancho)

½ teaspoon ground cinnamon

3-pound boneless pork shoulder

1½ teaspoons salt, plus more to taste

2 tablespoons canola oil

1 medium onion, chopped

1 to 2 garlic cloves, chopped

1 chipotle pepper in adobo sauce, chopped, plus 1 tablespoon sauce

12-ounce beer (lager or ale works well)

28-ounce can crushed tomatoes

¼ cup orange juice

1 **Prep the pork.** Mix the cumin, chile powder, and cinnamon together in a small bowl and set aside. Remove the netting from the pork and trim the meat of any large chunks of fat. Cut the pork into 2-inch chunks, place in a large bowl, and rub with the salt and spice mix. Cover and refrigerate overnight. Remove from the refrigerator 30 minutes before cooking.

2 **Sear the pork.** Heat the oven to 300°F. Heat the oil in a large dutch oven over medium-high to high heat. When the oil shimmers, brown the meat on all sides, about 10 minutes total. Adjust the heat as needed. Transfer pork to a plate and cover with foil.

3 **Cook the aromatics.** Reduce the heat to medium and add the onions and a pinch of salt. Cook, stirring, until the onions soften and turn translucent, 2 to 3 minutes. Add the garlic, chipotle pepper, and adobo sauce and cook, stirring, for another 1 to 2 minutes.

4 **Add liquid.** Add the beer and nudge the heat up just a bit to medium-high. Cook, stirring, for another 2 to 3 minutes, scraping any browned bits off of the bottom of the pan. Add the tomatoes and orange juice and bring to a boil.

5 **Braise.** Turn off the heat, return the pork to the pot, cover, and place in the oven. Braise until the meat easily pulls apart with a fork, about 3 hours.

6 **Remove pot from the oven.** Let the pork cool in the pot, uncovered, for at least 30 minutes. Once cool, you can also put the entire pot, covered, in the fridge for up to a week, then proceed with the recipe as follows.

7 **Finish the sauce.** Place pork on a cutting board, wipe off and discard any fat that's accumulated on the surface, and cover loosely with foil. Skim the fat from the top of the braising liquid and discard. Set the pot back on the stove over medium heat, purée the liquid with an immersion blender, and simmer to warm the sauce.

8 **Pull the pork.** Using 2 forks or your hands, pull the pork apart into rope-like pieces. Discard any big chunks of fat that remain. Return 2 cups of the pork to the pot and stir to combine. (Refrigerate remaining pork in braising liquid for another night.) Taste and adjust seasoning as needed. Keep warm over low heat.

9 **Serve.** Serve with a scoop of creamy polenta (pg. 243), a drizzle of the braising liquid and some fresh parsley.

POLENTA TWO WAYS

15 MINUTES ACTIVE, 40 MINUTES TOTAL · *makes 8 cups*

THERE ARE TIMES when nothing but a bowl of soft, creamy polenta will do—it's the ultimate comfort food. But once it's cooled, it's hard to recreate that consistency. So I embrace the polenta square. Crisped up in the oven, it gets a little crunch on the exterior but stays pillowy inside.

2 cups coarse ground cornmeal

2 to 3 tablespoons butter

Salt, to taste

Freshly ground black pepper, to taste

1 **Cook the polenta.** Bring 8 cups of salted water to boil in a large saucepan. Add the cornmeal in a steady stream, whisking as you go. Adjust the heat to medium and cook, stirring, for 10 to 15 minutes. Turn heat down to low and partially cover the pot, stirring occasionally for the next 20 minutes or so. When the polenta looks smooth and starts to pull away from the sides of the pot, it's ready.

2 **Finish and reserve half.** Stir in the butter and season to taste with salt and pepper. Pour half of the polenta into a baking dish and cool before covering and refrigerating for later use. Keep remaining polenta over low heat until you're ready to serve, stirring occasionally to keep polenta from sticking to the bottom of the pot.

The Standard

THESE MEATBALLS ARE IN OUR REGULAR ROTATION in fall and winter. Their origin is a Marcella Hazan recipe, but like all longstanding dishes in my arsenal, I tweak according to what's on hand, my mood, and my audience. These are super kid-friendly, easy to put together, and make the simplest meal feel special. The polenta squares are a great pasta substitute for those nights when you just can't face another noodle. Serve them alongside some Lemon-Garlic Broccoli (pg. 273) or another vegetable of your choice.

This recipe creates a light tomato sauce that just coats the meatballs. For a heartier sauce, take the meatballs out of the pan after browning them. Sauté half a chopped onion, a clove of chopped garlic, and a teaspoon of tomato paste in the tablespoon of oil remaining in the pan, then add a second cup of crushed tomatoes and simmer for ten minutes before adding the meatballs back to the pan.

I often double (or even triple) the meatball recipe, because let's face it: it's never a bad thing to have meatballs waiting in the freezer. You can freeze them raw (individually on a sheet pan, then store in a freezer bag once they've hardened); or directly in the sauce. They'll keep in the freezer for up to six months, but I like to use them within a month.

Marcella's Meatballs with Polenta Squares

30 MINUTES ACTIVE, 45 MINUTES TOTAL · *serves 4*

1 batch firm **POLENTA**

2 tablespoons canola oil

1 slice slightly stale bread, crusts removed, crumbled (use what you have)

⅓ cup milk

¼ medium yellow onion, finely chopped

4 tablespoons finely grated parmesan, plus more for garnish

1 garlic clove, chopped

3 tablespoons chopped parsley

1 egg

1 pound ground beef

1 scant teaspoon salt, plus more to taste

½ teaspoon freshly ground black pepper, plus more to taste

¼ teaspoon ground nutmeg

1 cup crushed tomatoes

1 **Prepare the polenta squares.** Heat the oven to 400°F. Cut 4 squares, about 3x3 inches each, from the pan of polenta and transfer to an oiled baking sheet. Brush the tops with oil and place in the oven until they're crisp on the outside and warmed through, about 20 minutes.

2 **Make the meatballs.** Place the bread in a medium bowl and pour the milk over it to soak. After 10 minutes, add the onions, parmesan, garlic, parsley, and egg and stir to combine. Add the beef and gently break it up in the bowl with a wooden spoon or your hands, mixing to combine all of the ingredients. Add the salt, pepper, and nutmeg and mix to combine once again. To taste the seasoning, cook a small patty in a hot skillet. Adjust seasoning as needed.

3 **Pan-fry.** Oil your hands and gently form the mixture into 16 1-ounce rounds (about the size of golf balls). Heat a large skillet or sauté pan over medium heat and add the oil. When the oil shimmers, slip the meatballs into the skillet in a single layer. Cook undisturbed for about 5 minutes. When they lift easily off of the bottom of the pan, flip and brown for another 3 to 5 minutes.

4 **Add the tomatoes.** Drain all but one tablespoon of oil from the pan. Add the tomatoes and bring to a simmer over medium heat. Reduce heat to low, cover, cook for another 10 minutes, and season sauce to taste. If storing, remove pan from heat and let meatballs and sauce cool before transferring to a storage container.

5 **Serve.** If you've made the meatballs ahead of time, gently warm them in their sauce in a saucepan over medium-low heat. Spoon 3 to 4 meatballs with their sauce over each polenta square. Serve alongside a zippy vegetable dish like the Lemon-Garlic Broccoli (pg. 273).

Pulled Pork Sandwiches • Red Cabbage Slaw

15 MINUTES ACTIVE, 30 MINUTES TOTAL • *serves 4*

TONIGHT, WE SHALL EAT DELICIOUS PULLED PORK SANDWICHES. You've done the hard work already, now you just need something crunchy to go along with it. This colorful slaw can be dressed up to a day ahead of time. Pile it up!

RED CABBAGE SLAW

½ medium head red cabbage, cored and thinly sliced

1 teaspoon salt, plus more to taste

2 to 3 medium carrots, peeled and grated

2 tablespoons granulated sugar

2 tablespoons cider vinegar

¼ cup chopped scallion greens

¼ cup chopped cilantro

PULLED PORK SANDWICHES

2 cups **BRAISED PORK**

4 sandwich buns (I like Martin's potato buns)

½ cup **PICKLED RED ONIONS** (pg. 270), roughly chopped

1 **Salt the cabbage.** In a large bowl, toss the cabbage and salt together. Let it sit for about 30 minutes, then transfer to a colander to drain. Press the cabbage down to squeeze out as much liquid as possible.

2 **Make the dressing.** Return the cabbage to the bowl and toss with the grated carrots. In a small bowl, whisk together the sugar and vinegar, then pour it over the slaw and toss to combine. Add more sugar, salt, or vinegar to taste. If you're making the slaw ahead, you can stop here until you're ready to serve.

3 **Prep the pork.** Place the pork and some of its braising liquid in a small saucepan and warm it over low heat. Once the pork is warm, transfer to a cutting board and chop or pull it into bite-size pieces.

4 **Assemble and serve.** Add the scallion greens and cilantro to the slaw and toss well. Divide the pork evenly among the 4 buns and top each with a sprinkle of chopped pickled red onions. Serve with slaw, either as a side or piled on top of the sandwiches.

Pub Grub

PRE-KIDS, I LEFT WINGS TO THE EXPERTS at the local pub. Turns out, these little guys are just right for my little guys—the stickier and messier the better. If you have time, salt the chicken the night before; if not, even thirty minutes will help.

BARBEQUE SAUCE

MAKE AHEAD!

30 MINUTES · *makes 1 cup*

2 teaspoons vegetable oil

1 tablespoon shredded red onion

1 garlic clove, peeled and shredded

1 tablespoon tomato paste

½ cup ketchup

¼ cup maple syrup

¼ cup cider vinegar

¼ cup soy sauce

2 tablespoons tamarind paste (optional)

Dash of hot pepper sauce (optional)

Heat the oil in a small saucepan over medium heat. Add the onion and garlic and cook until fragrant, 2 to 3 minutes. Add the tomato paste and cook, stirring, 3 minutes. Stir in the remaining ingredients and bring to a simmer. Reduce heat and simmer for about 20 minutes, stirring occasionally. Cool and transfer to a jar with a lid.

BBQ Wings · Oven Fries

45 MINUTES · *serves 4*

BBQ CHICKEN WINGS

1 pound chicken wings and drumettes

1 teaspoon salt

¼ cup **BARBEQUE SAUCE**

OVEN FRIES

4 potatoes

2 tablespoons olive oil

½ teaspoon salt

½ teaspoon paprika

1 **Prep.** If you haven't already, toss chicken with salt. Cut the potatoes lengthwise into 1/2-inch strips. Place in a bowl of cold water until ready to cook.

2 **Cook the wings.** Turn on the broiler. Place chicken on a rimmed baking sheet lined with foil and broil for 3 to 4 minutes. Flip and broil for another 3 to 4 minutes. Flip again and brush the wings with some of the sauce. Broil another 2 to 3 minutes. Flip and brush the other side with sauce, and broil for another 2 to 3 minutes. Remove from oven and set aside.

3 **Make the fries.** Drain the potatoes and thoroughly pat dry. Toss with olive oil and a sprinkle of the salt, place on a baking sheet, and roast, turning occasionally, for 30 minutes or until crispy.

4 **Finish and serve.** Return the wings to the oven for about 3 minutes before the potatoes are done to warm them up. Toss in a bowl with any remaining sauce. Remove potatoes and toss with remaining salt (plus more to taste) and paprika. Serve wings and potatoes together. I like to serve these with some sliced raw vegetables and a salty yogurt sauce for dipping.

Seared Scallops · Fettuccine with Spinach & Bacon

40 MINUTES · *serves 4*

SEA SCALLOPS BRING A LITTLE LUXURY to a weeknight dinner. Sweet and a wee bit briny, they're a special treat, and I try not to fuss with them too much. I just make sure that my pan is super hot and that my cooking fat can handle the heat. Since I'm cooking bacon anyway, I use bacon fat here; it has a high smoke point and makes everything taste delicious. Serve the scallops and greens on a nest of fettuccine (or alongside, for people who don't like their food to touch).

1 pound fettuccine

4 pieces thick-cut bacon, cut into ¼-inch pieces

1 tablespoon minced garlic

1½ pounds spinach

¼ teaspoon salt, plus more to taste

1 pound scallops, tough muscle removed

1 tablespoon bacon fat

1 tablespoon unsalted butter

Juice of ½ lemon

1 tablespoon minced chives

Freshly ground black pepper, to taste

1 **Cook the pasta.** Prepare fettuccine according to package directions. Drain, reserving ½ cup pasta water, rinse with cold water, and set aside.

2 **Prep the scallops.** Rinse the scallops under cold water and pat them dry. Set aside.

3 **Make the wilted spinach and bacon.** Place the bacon in large, heavy-bottomed skillet over low heat. Cook, stirring occasionally, until most of the fat has rendered and the bacon is brown, 7 to 10 minutes. Turn off heat and transfer bacon to a paper towel-lined plate. Drain bacon fat from the pan, reserving 1 tablespoon. Add the garlic and cook, stirring, for 1 minute. Add the spinach and salt and cook, stirring, for 3 to 5 minutes, until the spinach wilts and turns a deep green. Toss in bacon and stir to combine. Transfer to serving dish, cover, and set aside.

4 **Sear.** Wipe out the skillet and add 1 tablespoon bacon fat (if you didn't get enough fat from the rendered bacon, make up the difference with a neutral oil with a high smoke point, like safflower). Place the skillet over high heat. When the fat shimmers, add the scallops in a single layer. Sprinkle with a pinch of salt. Cook the scallops without disturbing until the side touching the skillet starts turning opaque, 2 to 3 minutes.

5 **Finish the pasta.** Get 4 shallow bowls ready for serving. Place the butter in a large skillet or dutch oven over medium heat. When it foams, add the pasta and toss until it is warmed through, drizzling in reserved pasta water and tossing to emulsify. Use tongs to transfer a nest of fettuccine to each bowl (you'll have pasta left over). Add the spinach and bacon mixture to the pasta pot and toss briefly to warm.

6 **Finish the scallops.** Flip the scallops, sprinkle with a pinch of salt, and cook for another 1 to 2 minutes. Turn off the heat. The scallops should be opaque and browned on both sides, but still tender inside.

7 **Serve.** Top each bowl of noodles with some of the spinach mixture, and then divide the scallops among the bowls. Finish with a squeeze of lemon, a sprinkle of chives, and a few grinds of black pepper.

GOOD GUESTING

A COUPLE OF TIMES A YEAR, we head west to visit friends and family who live around the Finger Lakes region in upstate New York. I love it here. If there were any place that could pry me from living close enough to the ocean to catch a whiff of it every now and then, this would be it.

Around Ithaca and Cayuga Lake, farming is alive and well. Our friends Deva and Eric live on ten acres with sheep and geese and an orchard filled with dozens of varieties of cider apples they press, bottle, and ferment into their magical Redbyrd Cider. Everywhere you look, there are cideries, wineries, dairies, and cheesemakers. It's easy to get your hands on locally raised meat of every kind, as well as grains grown and milled in the area. It seems like just about everyone up there grows a little something—hops or flowers or a few rows of vegetables—but their little something is a whole lot more than we can muster in our tiny Boston yard.

With all that agriculture, it's no surprise there's also lots of good food. We often stay with Galen's cousins, who are among the original founders of the Moosewood Collective. We eat well and often when visiting them—venison stew, eggs with bright orange yolks spilling over sausage-studded grits, fig and apple galettes, homemade pizza, the world's densest brownies. The best part? We like to talk about the next eating opportunity while we're digging into some rustic, delicious, and veggie-loaded meal.

It's not summer without a trip to upstate New York, but Thanksgiving there is also pretty special. To get to the Finger Lakes from Boston is a trek. With holiday traffic and two small kids who need frequent breaks from sitting, it can take over eight hours. So I tend not to bring what I'd usually bring to a Thanksgiving celebration closer to home—pie or some green vegetable tarted up in a vinaigrette. I focus on the other ways I can get invited back. We bring lots of beer. I call dish duty, prep duty, whatever duty is needed, including keeping my kids as mellow as possible duty. And if I really have my act together, I'll bring a beautiful ripe wheel of cheese (Jasper Hill's Harbison tends to delight people) and a big bag of granola to share at breakfast.

Maple-Almond Granola

1 HOUR · *makes about 10 cups*

4 cups rolled oats

1 cup coconut flakes

1 cup sliced or slivered almonds

½ cup sunflower seeds

½ cup sesame seeds

1½ teaspoons salt

1 teaspoon ground ginger

1 teaspoon ground cardamom

½ cup maple syrup

2 tablespoons golden syrup or corn syrup (to help the mixture clump and stick together)

1 cup chopped dried apricots

1   **Make the granola.** Heat the oven to 300°F (or 275°F, if your oven runs hot) and line 2 baking sheets with parchment paper. Toss together all of the ingredients except the syrups and apricots in a large bowl. Add the syrups and mix until well combined (here's where rolling up the sleeves really comes into play). Spread the granola evenly onto the baking sheets.

2   **Bake.** Place baking sheets in the oven and bake for 30 minutes, then rotate the sheets so the granola browns evenly. Continue baking for another 20 to 25 minutes, until the granola is a medium caramel color. Cool completely before breaking up and stirring in the apricots.

3   **Store.** Transfer to a storage container with a lid. The granola will keep, covered, for a week. To give as a gift, scoop 2 to 3 cups into a clear cellophane gift bag, write the ingredients on a gift tag, and tie with raffia or baker's twine.

December

SESAME-GINGER MEATBALLS WITH BOK CHOY

BLACK BEAN SOUP • ROASTED DELICATA SQUASH

DIY SWEET POTATOES

SHRIMP & GRITS

LEMON JUMBLES

THERE'S NO GETTING AROUND IT: December is a hectic month. Part of the frenzy is all that holiday-related fun… but still. I spend a lot of time staring at my calendar and making lists of the lists I need to make. Planning our dinners helps me keep the chaos at bay, so I make sure it happens, even if the plans are super simple. I only gave you four dinner ideas this week; do yourself a favor and call for delivery one night. What can I say? I'm a realist.

WHEN THE WEEKENDS FILL UP, I still try to find a few hours to prep meal components to keep dinnertime streamlined during the week. If I don't get a chance to do much, I count on mealtime taking longer in the evening, so I make sure we have some quick snacks on hand to curb the hangries (cue the beet hummus, pg. 279). I balance those efforts with something speedy the next evening and earn back enough time to knock a few more holiday-related things off the to-do list.

Budget a few hours over the weekend to prep for this week's menu. Start by soaking the black beans overnight, then set them simmering with a ham hock to make a simple but flavorful soup that will take you far with leftovers. While that's on the back burner, make the sesame-ginger meatballs for that evening's rice bowls. (Consider making a double batch of both the meatballs and the rice—you'll be happy you did.) Finish up with the sautéed bok choy and make time to sit down together for a family meal.

Later in the week, help yourself out and bake the sweet potatoes in advance. They take up to an hour to cook, but they're minimal work, making meal prep a breeze.

THE BIG COOK

SOAK THE BLACK BEANS AND MAKE THE SOUP

MAKE A BATCH (OR TWO!) OF THE MEATBALLS AND FREEZE ANY EXTRAS

STEAM THE BROWN RICE

OTHER WAYS TO GET AHEAD

BAKE THE SWEET POTATOES

Sesame-Ginger Meatballs with Bok Choy

1 HOUR ACTIVE, 2 HOURS TOTAL · *serves 4 to 6*

THESE MEATBALLS are one of the best uses of ground turkey I've discovered yet. One batch usually serves my family of four with a few left for someone's lunch the next day (mine, thanks!).

Two cups of rice is a double batch, so you'll likely have some left for another meal. You can also double the meatballs—they're easy to freeze. Put them right on the sheet pan, place the pan in the freezer, then transfer to a labeled freezer bag when they've hardened. For their next act, try them in a banh mi-style sandwich (pg. 59), or in a brothy udon soup (pg. 56).

RICE

2 cups short-grain brown rice

SESAME-GINGER MEATBALLS

2 tablespoons sesame seeds

1 scallion, white and light green parts, minced

2-inch piece ginger, peeled and grated

2 garlic cloves, chopped

1 teaspoon dark brown sugar

½ teaspoon sriracha

1 pound ground turkey

1 tablespoon soy sauce

1 teaspoon fish sauce (optional, but delicious!)

1 egg, lightly beaten

½ teaspoon salt, plus more to taste

3 to 4 tablespoons panko crumbs

HONEY-SOY SAUCE

¼ cup soy sauce

2 tablespoons rice wine vinegar

1-inch piece ginger, sliced into coins

2 tablespoons honey

BOK CHOY

1 tablespoon vegetable oil

4 small or 2 medium heads bok choy, split in half vertically and trimmed

1 medium garlic clove, chopped

2 tablespoons soy sauce

GARNISHES

Thinly sliced radishes

Chopped scallion greens

Sesame seeds

Cilantro

Sriracha

1 **Make the rice.** Once rice has fully absorbed water, turn off the heat and leave covered until ready to serve.

2 **Make the meatballs.** Combine sesame seeds, scallions, ginger, garlic, sugar, sriracha, and turkey together in a medium bowl. Stir until all ingredients are combined. Add the soy sauce, fish sauce, egg, and salt and stir to combine. Add the panko, a tablespoon at a time, depending on how wet the mixture is (it will firm up when it chills, so don't go nuts with the panko or the meatballs will be spongy), and combine one last time. To taste the seasoning, cook a small patty in an oiled skillet. Adjust seasoning as needed.

3 **Form the meatballs.** Line a rimmed baking sheet with parchment paper. Form the meat into 1-ounce rounds (about the size of golf balls) and refrigerate on the baking sheet for at least 30 minutes (if making a double batch, you can freeze half now).

4 **Bake.** A few minutes before you're ready to bake, heat the oven to 425°F. Remove meatballs from the refrigerator and bake until cooked through, about 15 minutes.

5 **Make the sauce.** While the meatballs are baking, whisk together the soy sauce, vinegar, ¼ cup water, ginger, and honey in a medium bowl. Add to a large saucepan, bring to medium heat and cook, stirring to combine. Bring to a simmer in a large saucepan over medium heat and cook, stirring occasionally, until the sauce turns syrupy, about 10 minutes. Discard the ginger. Keep warm over low heat. When the meatballs come out of the oven, add them to the saucepan and lightly toss to coat them in the sauce. Keep warm.

6 **Cook the bok choy.** Add the oil to a medium sauté pan over medium heat. Add the bok choy and garlic and cook, stirring, for 1 minute. Add ¼ cup water and the soy sauce and bring to a boil. Toss to coat the bok choy, reduce heat to medium-low, and cover. Cook until tender, about 5 minutes, then uncover and continue cooking until the liquid evaporates. Remove from heat.

7 **Serve.** Fluff the rice with a fork. Place a scoop of rice in each bowl. Add the meatballs, sauce, and bok choy. Garnish each bowl with a few radish slices, chopped scallions, a sprinkle of sesame seeds, a few cilantro leaves, and sriracha and serve.

Cook, Eat, Repeat

WHEN I WAS IN COLLEGE, one of my housemates went through a protracted split pea soup phase. Back then, I never cooked the same thing twice and couldn't quite wrap my head around her habit. But lately, as I try to simplify so many aspects of life and still eat delicious things, I can see where she was coming from.

This black bean soup—rich, warming, and economical—makes the case for this kind of cooking. Pulling this soup from the freezer in anticipation of a rushed and busy weeknight always makes me feel like I'm getting away with something.

If you double the recipe, you can still just use one ham hock—they have plenty of flavor to spare.

BLACK BEAN SOUP   MAKE AHEAD!

30 MINUTES ACTIVE, 4 HOURS TOTAL · *serves 6 to 8*

2 tablespoons olive oil	2 medium garlic cloves, chopped
1 to 2 medium yellow onions, chopped	1 pound dry **BLACK BEANS**, soaked overnight and drained
1 teaspoon salt, plus more to taste	1 ham hock
1 teaspoon dried chile powder (I use ancho)	2 bay leaves
1 tablespoon tomato paste	Juice of 1 orange
1 chipotle pepper in adobo sauce, chopped, plus 1 tablespoon sauce	2 tablespoons red wine vinegar

1   **Sauté the onions and spices.** In a large, heavy-bottomed pot, heat the oil over medium heat. When it shimmers, add the onions and a pinch of salt and cook, stirring, for 3 to 5 minutes, until the onions soften. Add the chile powder, tomato paste, and chipotle in adobo sauce and cook, stirring, for 3 to 4 more minutes. Add the garlic and cook, stirring, for 2 to 3 more minutes.

2   **Add the beans and ham hock.** Fill a pot with enough water to cover beans by 1 inch. Bring to a boil, and then reduce heat to a simmer. Skim any foam that rises to the top of the pot.

3   **Simmer.** Add the bay leaves and simmer until the beans are tender and glossy, about 3 hours. Stir occasionally, adding water as needed to keep things soupy.

4   **Remove the ham hock from the pot.** When it is cool enough to handle, pull the meat from the bone, chop the meat, and return it to the soup.

5   **Finish the soup.** Stir in the orange juice, vinegar, and a sprinkle of salt and simmer for 12 to 15 minutes more. Taste and add more salt if needed. Once cool, soup can be stored for up to 5 days in the refrigerator or 6 months in the freezer (I like to use it within 2 months).

Black Bean Soup · Roasted Delicata Squash

30 MINUTES · *serves 4*

DELICATA SQUASH

1 to 2 small delicata squash, halved vertically, seeded, and cut into ¼-inch slices

1 to 2 tablespoons olive oil

½ teaspoon salt

½ teaspoon light brown sugar

½ teaspoon ground cumin

SOUP & GARNISHES

BLACK BEAN SOUP

8 corn tortillas

3 to 4 tablespoons chopped cilantro (use some for the roasted squash, too)

Plain yogurt or sour cream

Toasted pumpkin seeds

Chopped scallions

Avocado slices

Lime wedges

1 **Roast the squash.** Heat the oven to 400°F. Toss the sliced squash, olive oil, salt, sugar, and cumin together on a rimmed baking sheet. Roast until squash browns and starts to crisp at the edges, about 25 minutes.

2 **Serve.** If needed, reheat the soup in a saucepan over medium-low heat. Warm the tortillas and cover with a towel. Serve the soup with tortillas, garnishes, and roasted squash.

DIY Sweet Potatoes

30 MINUTES ACTIVE, 1 HOUR TOTAL · *serves 4*

DIY MEALS JUST MAKE A LOT OF SENSE in my household. Kids can customize to their hearts' content and it allows me to move odds and ends out of the fridge. If I have random bits of cheeses, ham, or some mushrooms that need to get cooked and eaten, they get added to the array of toppings. Leftover black bean soup from earlier in the week? Add it to the table! Sweet potatoes make for a nutrient-rich base for all those fun bits and bobs (plus they taste like vegetable candy). I like to serve this with a big green salad, like my go-to Autumn Salad (pg. 275). You can throw the potatoes in the oven the moment you step into the house and have dinner an hour later, or bake the spuds in advance and cut your night-of meal prep time by more than half.

4 sweet potatoes

Olive oil, for rubbing on the potatoes

TOPPING IDEAS

1 cup **BLACK BEAN SOUP**, reheated on the stove

2 to 3 scallions, green parts only, chopped

1 avocado, pitted and chopped into ½-inch pieces

½ cup yogurt

½ cup shredded cheese

Little cubes of ham or strips of salami

Sautéed greens

Sautéed mushrooms

Corn kernels

Salsa verde

Pumpkin seeds

1 **Bake the potatoes.** Heat the oven to 375°F. Prick the sweet potatoes all over with a fork, rub them with a bit of olive oil, and put them on a sheet pan in the oven. Bake until tender when pierced with a fork, 40 to 60 minutes (depending on their size). Store the potatoes in foil in the refrigerator until ready to use, up to 3 days. To reheat, warm them in a 350°F oven for 15 to 20 minutes before serving.

2 **Serve.** Split open the sweet potatoes and serve with a wide variety of toppings. Serve the salad alongside.

Shrimp & Grits

25 MINUTES ACTIVE, 45 MINUTES TOTAL · *serves 4*

DELICIOUS AND SUPER SATISFYING, this is a meal that comes together easily but still feels special. Serve it with a quick salad or garlicky tender greens (pg. 271).

I'm picky about these critters—my preference is wild-caught, domestic shrimp, which isn't always available. So when I see them in the market, I pounce and stash them in the freezer. I'll admit it's a pain to peel and devein them yourself, but if you find shell-on shrimp, you can use the shells for a quick and simple stock that you can incorporate in this recipe or freeze and use the next time you're making fish soup or stew. Place the shells in a medium saucepan, cover with water by an inch, and add a couple of lemon slices, a bay leaf or two, a scattering of peppercorns, and a quarter of an onion. Bring to a bare simmer and cook, stirring occasionally (don't let it boil), for 10 to 15 minutes. Strain out the solids and use here or freeze for later. You can also freeze the shells and pull them out to make stock another time.

GRITS

1 cup stone-ground grits

1 teaspoon salt, plus
    more to taste

1 tablespoon butter

SHRIMP

4 slices thick-cut bacon,
    cut into ¼-inch pieces

24 large shrimp, peeled
    and deveined

Salt, to taste

Freshly ground black
    pepper, to taste

½ yellow onion, chopped

1 garlic clove, chopped

½ cup chicken or shrimp
    stock (see headnote)

1 tablespoon lemon juice

1 tablespoon unsalted
    butter

Tabasco sauce, to taste

½ cup chopped scallions

1 **Make the grits.** Bring 4 cups water to a boil in a medium saucepan. Whisk in the grits and a pinch of salt. (I find that continuous whisking in the beginning means you don't have to stir the grits throughout.) Whisk until the mixture bubbles and thickens, then reduce heat to medium-low and cook, stirring occasionally, until the grits fully absorb the water and pull away from the sides of the pot, about 20 minutes. Stir in the butter. Taste and adjust seasoning. Keep warm over low heat, stirring occasionally.

2 **Cook the shrimp.** Place the bacon in large, heavy-bottomed skillet over medium heat. Cook, stirring occasionally, until most of the fat has rendered and the bacon is brown, 7 to 10 minutes. Turn off heat and transfer bacon to a paper towel-lined plate. Drain bacon fat from the pan, reserving 1 tablespoon for another use. Season the shrimp with a sprinkle of salt and pepper. Return the skillet to medium heat and add them to the pan. Cook, turning once, for 2 to 3 minutes on each side, depending on the size of the shrimp. They should be pink, but not totally opaque, after you've seared them.

3 **Make the sauce.** Transfer shrimp to a plate, reduce heat just a nudge, and add the onion and garlic to the pan. Cook, stirring, until the onions and garlic soften, 3 to 5 minutes, adding up to a tablespoon of the stock to keep things from sticking. Add the remaining stock, increase heat to medium-high, and cook, stirring, until the stock has reduced by half, another 3 to 4 minutes. Reduce heat to medium and return shrimp to the pan. Cook, stirring, for 1 to 2 minutes, then add the lemon juice, butter, and Tabasco. Cook, stirring, until sauce has thickened, 1 to 2 minutes more.

4 **Finish and serve.** Reheat the grits if necessary, stirring until they're warmed through. Divide grits between bowls, then top with the shrimp and sauce. Garnish with bacon, chopped scallions, and a few grinds of pepper.

HOLIDAY BAKING

HOLIDAY COOKIES ARE KIND OF MY THING. For years, when my friend Heather threw our annual (elaborate) holiday party, I always made multiple kinds of fussy cookies. One year, I sold them in a seasonal mail-order shop called Good Egg Cookies + Confections, making gift boxes of four different precious little treats. The boxes sold mostly to my mother, my mother-in-law, and their friends, but there were many joyous late nights making toffee that would eventually get ground up and sprinkled over chocolate-caramel sandwich cookies.

Then I had kids. And my cookie-baking goals shifted a bit. As a mom who loves baking, I had romantic visions of rolling dough with my boys, all calm and patient while they artfully sprinkled colored sugar over their seasonally appropriate cookies. The idea of baking with my children is a lovely one, but I have to admit the reality is slightly less rosy. I bicker with them over which shape cookie cutter to use (I say stars; they say dinosaurs). I bite my lip when they dump five different colors of sugar onto the same cookie. When you're a cookie control freak, relaxing in this scenario takes some work. And some deep breathing. Let's just say I'm working on it. (Note: It does get easier.)

But this is only one kind of holiday baking. The other kind is a late night session with just me, a boatload of butter, and a clutch of my favorite cookie recipes. Some are a little more prosaic than in years past, but I always include this one; it's unusual, delicious, and only a tiny bit fussy. These Lemon Jumbles are from *The All-American Cookie Book* by Nancy Baggett. I've made many recipes from her book and she's never steered me wrong, but this is the one I always return to. It was there on those cookie platters years ago, and it's remained on the holiday agenda ever since, even when I don't think I have any holiday baking bandwidth left.

....

BUILDING BAKING BANDWIDTH

Around here, the holidays are filled with important rituals. But between work and the kids' schedules, it can be a challenge to squeeze everything in—and the last thing I want is to pile on the stress during an already busy season. So I typically enter December with a plan in place to maintain the Christmas cookie ritual without losing my mind. The first thing I do is prioritize. I may not make my own wreaths, but cookies are here to stay. Here's how I make sure it goes smoothly:

- Choose the recipes (in November) and generate a master shopping list.

- Shop for all the ingredients in one day; make cookies another day.

- Block out baking time on the calendar.

- Store butter outside of the fridge so it's always soft and ready to go when needed. I keep mine on the windowsill.

- Make the dough for each cookie all in one session. Wrap tightly, label, and refrigerate.

- Find shorter chunks of time to bake and decorate the cookies, a few dozen at a time.

- Store finished cookies in the freezer and pull out assortments for whatever occasion they're needed.

Nancy Baggett's Lemon Jumbles

1 HOUR ACTIVE, 2 HOURS TOTAL · *makes 48 cookies*

COOKIES

2¾ cups all-purpose flour

1 teaspoon cream of tartar

½ teaspoon baking soda

¼ teaspoon salt

1 cup (2 sticks) unsalted butter, at room temperature

Scant 1 cup granulated sugar

1 large egg

1 tablespoon lemon juice

1 tablespoon finely grated lemon zest

1 teaspoon almond extract

GLAZE

1½ cups powdered sugar

1 tablespoon unsalted butter, softened

1 to 2 tablespoons lemon juice

½ teaspoon light corn syrup

2 drops almond extract

¼ cup blanched sliced almonds

1 **Get ready.** Heat the oven to 350°F. Line 2 rimmed baking sheets with parchment paper.

2 **Make the dough.** In a large bowl, stir together the flour, cream of tartar, baking soda, and salt and set aside. In a stand mixer fitted with the paddle attachment, cream together the butter and sugar on medium speed until smooth, 1 to 2 minutes. Add the egg, lemon juice and zest, and almond extract and mix until well-blended and smooth. Add the dry ingredients a little bit at a time and mix until all ingredients are fully incorporated.

3 **Shape the cookies.** Turn the dough out onto a floured work surface and gather it into a ball. Quarter the dough and shape each quarter into a flat round. Score each round into quarters, then cut each round into 12 pieces. On the work surface, roll each piece into a 4 to 5 inch rope, then join the ends of the rope to form a ring. Pinch the dough together to adhere the ends.

4 **Bake.** Place the rings on the baking sheets and bake, one sheet at a time on a rack in the center of the oven, for 8 to 12 minutes. Rotate the baking sheets halfway through to ensure even browning. The cookies should be golden and lightly browned on the edges. Transfer to a cooling rack and cool completely before glazing.

5 **Glaze.** In a small bowl, whisk together all of the ingredients except the almonds until the mixture forms a smooth glaze. Thin with additional lemon juice if the mix seems too thick. Set the cooling racks over a piece of parchment or wax paper to catch drips. Dip the top of each cookie into the glaze, letting any excess drip back into the bowl. Dip 3 or 4 cookies at a time, then sprinkle with the almonds and return to the cooling rack. Repeat with the remaining cookies. Let sit until the glaze dries completely, about an hour.

6 **Store.** The cookies will keep in an airtight container for about 2 weeks or in the freezer for up to 2 months. They thaw quickly, so I often make them early in the holiday season, keep the batch in freezer bags, and pull out what I need for different occasions.

Standards & Twists

SUCCESSFUL WEEKNIGHT DINNERS are all about strategizing. You're short on time and energy, so you need to figure out (preferably in advance) where to focus your efforts. Over the years of cooking for a family of four, I have learned to focus my energy on a well-balanced central dish and keep the sides simple if I make them at all. In part this is because I know I can't do it all (and I also don't want to clean it all), and it's easier to get my boys to embrace vegetables when they're at their most basic—raw, roasted, steamed, or pickled.

This chapter highlights some of those vegetable basics, along with a few other workhorse items that are in constant rotation in my kitchen—building block-type stuff that gives me components for dinner, snacks, and other meals, too.

PICKLED VEGETABLES

AS IT TURNS OUT, most vegetables respond well to being soaked in brine. And once you get in the habit, making a few quick pickles is an easy way to introduce some pretty dynamic flavors to your family meals. Here are some of the most common pickles I make. Once you're used to the general process, you can try just about anything—radishes or turnips instead of carrots, seasonal vegetables like asparagus, different types of chiles, fruit (!), and more.

Pickled Red Onions

20 MINUTES ACTIVE, AT LEAST 90 MINUTES TO BRINE
makes 1 pint

1 medium red onion, peeled, halved, and cut into ¼-inch slices

1 to 2 bay leaves

1 to 2 thyme sprigs

¾ cup distilled white vinegar

¼ cup apple cider vinegar

2 tablespoons granulated sugar

2 teaspoons salt

¼ teaspoon whole black peppercorns

¼ teaspoon fennel seeds

Add onions, bay leaves, and thyme to a glass pint jar with a lid. In a small saucepan, bring remaining ingredients to a simmer over medium heat. Simmer, stirring occasionally, until salt and sugar have dissolved.

Pour hot brine over the onions and let sit for 30 minutes. Cover and refrigerate for at least 1 hour or overnight. These will keep in the refrigerator for 2 to 3 weeks.

Pickled Carrots

20 MINUTES ACTIVE, AT LEAST 90 MINUTES TO BRINE
makes 1 pint

2 medium carrots, peeled and sliced into thin coins

1-inch piece of ginger, sliced into thin coins

¾ cup distilled white vinegar

¼ cup rice wine vinegar

2 tablespoons granulated sugar

2 teaspoons salt

¼ teaspoon coriander seeds

¼ teaspoon whole black peppercorns

Add carrots and ginger to a glass pint jar with a lid. In a small saucepan, bring remaining ingredients to a simmer over medium heat. Simmer, stirring occasionally, until salt and sugar have dissolved.

Pour hot brine over the carrots and let sit for 30 minutes. Cover and refrigerate for at least 1 hour or overnight. These will keep in the refrigerator for 2 to 3 weeks.

Pickled Jalapeños

20 MINUTES ACTIVE, AT LEAST 90 MINUTES TO BRINE
makes 1 pint

6 to 8 medium jalapeños, sliced into ¼-inch rings

2 medium cloves garlic, peeled and lightly crushed

¾ cup distilled white vinegar

¼ cup rice wine vinegar

2 tablespoons granulated sugar

2 teaspoons salt

¼ teaspoon coriander seeds

¼ teaspoon fennel seeds

Add jalapeños and garlic to a glass pint jar with a lid. In a small saucepan, bring remaining ingredients to a simmer over medium heat. Simmer, stirring occasionally, until salt and sugar have dissolved.

Pour hot brine over the jalapeños and let sit for 30 minutes. Cover and refrigerate for at least 1 hour or overnight. These will keep in the refrigerator for 2 to 3 weeks.

SIMPLE GREENS

KIDS WON'T EAT THEIR GREENS? Shocker. When it comes to the leafy stuff, I think it never hurts to just keep trying. And again, I like to keep it simple. Below is a template for sautéed greens—you can use tender chard, beet greens, spinach, or slightly heartier kale or collards. Improvise with the aromatics you add at the beginning (I like to add some minced anchovy to my kale, but please don't tell my kids) and the way you finish them at the end (stir that last splash of heavy cream into the spinach, you won't hate it).

One of the nice things about cooked greens is they transition well into another meal. Throw them into your breakfast tacos, grain bowls, soup, or pressed sandwiches the next day.

Sautéed Tender Greens

15 MINUTES · *serves 4*

1 tablespoon olive oil

1 garlic clove, peeled and minced

1 pound chard, spinach, or beet leaves, torn into 1-inch pieces

Pinch of salt

Red pepper flakes

Pinch of freshly ground black pepper (optional)

Lemon wedge

Place the olive oil in a medium skillet over medium-low heat. Add the garlic and cook, stirring, for 1 to 2 minutes. Add the greens, stir to coat with the oil, and cook until wilted, 3 to 4 minutes depending on how tender the greens are. Sprinkle with salt, optional peppers, and a squeeze of lemon.

Sautéed Hearty Greens

20 MINUTES · *serves 4*

1 tablespoon olive oil, plus more for drizzling

1 garlic clove, peeled and minced

1 pound kale, collard, or turnip greens, stemmed and torn into 1-inch pieces

¼ cup water or stock

Pinch of salt

Freshly ground black pepper, to taste

Pinch of red pepper flakes, optional

Splash of red wine vinegar

Place the oil in a large sauté pan over medium-low heat. Add the garlic and cook, stirring, for 1 to 2 minutes. Add the greens and stir to coat in the olive oil. Add the water, stir to coat, increase the heat to medium-high, and cover. Cook until the greens have wilted and most of the liquid has evaporated, 3 to 4 minutes. Reduce heat to low and stir in a pinch of salt, a few grinds of pepper, and optional pepper flakes. Stir in a splash of vinegar and finish with a drizzle of olive oil.

STURDY VEG

WHETHER YOU ARE roasting, grilling, or steaming, batch cooking vegetables also gives you the chance to improvise—tonight's leftover lemon-garlic broccoli might turn into tomorrow's broccoli salad with chickpeas and tahini dressing, or extra green beans might get an Asian-style treatment when you have stir fry a few nights later.

Blanching vegetables is a great way to extend their life in the refrigerator and speed dinner time up. To blanch your green vegetables, fill a pot with cold water, add enough salt to make it briny, cover, and bring to a boil. When the water is boiling, submerge the vegetables and cook until bright green, about 3 minutes. Drain and plunge into cold water to stop the cooking. Pat dry and store.

Peppers:
Grilled, Broiled, or Roasted

On the grill: Light a charcoal or gas grill to medium-high heat. Place the peppers on the grill and cook, turning occasionally, until the skins blacken and the peppers soften and collapse, about 10 minutes.

In the oven: Place peppers on a foil-lined sheet-pan. The quickest method is to run them under the broiler for about 10-12 minutes, monitoring their progress and flipping every few minutes. If you're roasting other vegetables at the same time, roast for 30-40 minutes, until skin starts to blacken.

For all methods: Remove from heat, transfer to a bowl, cover with plastic wrap, and set aside for about 10 minutes to cool and let the skins loosen. When cool enough to touch, remove the skin and seeds. Store in the fridge for about a week.

Roasted Beets

5 MINUTES ACTIVE, 60 MINUTES TOTAL

5 to 10 beets

1 to 2 tablespoons olive oil

1 teaspoons salt

Preheat the oven to 375°F.

Place 5 medium or 10 small, unpeeled beets in a sheet pan or baking dish, drizzle with olive oil, sprinkle with salt, shake to coat, and add enough water to come up the sides of the dish by ¼ inch. Cover with foil and steam-roast in the oven until the beets are easily pricked with a knife or fork, 50 to 60 minutes.

After they've cooled, transfer the beets to a storage container and keep them in the fridge until it's time to use them—whether for a dinner salad, puréed into hummus, sliced and sautéed with butter, cider vinegar, and chives for a dinner side, or chopped into a hearty grain salad for lunch. They keep longer if you leave the skins on; just remove them right before you slice them up.

Roasted Red Peppers and Carrots with Feta

5 MINUTES · *serves 4*

3 roasted carrots, cut into ½-inch slices

2 roasted red peppers, roughly chopped

½ cup parsley leaves

2 tablespoons olive oil

Salt, to taste

2 teaspoons sherry vinegar

2 ounces sheep's milk feta, crumbled

Freshly ground black pepper, to taste

Toss the carrots with the peppers and parsley leaves. Add the olive oil, season to taste with salt, and toss again. Add the vinegar, toss to coat, and season to taste once more if needed. Finish with crumbled feta and a few grinds of black pepper.

Lemon-Garlic Broccoli

15 TO 20 MINUTES · *serves 4*

1 pound broccoli, stems peeled, blanched, and cut into 1-inch pieces

3 tablespoons olive oil

Zest and juice of 1 lemon

2 garlic cloves, peeled and minced

Coarse salt, to taste

Freshly ground black pepper, to taste

Fill a medium pot with cold water, add ½ teaspoon salt, cover, and bring to a boil.

Heat the oil in a skillet over medium heat. Add the lemon zest, garlic, and a pinch of salt and cook, stirring, for about 1 minute, until fragrant. Add the broccoli and stir to coat. Cook, stirring, for 2 to 3 minutes. Add the lemon juice and stir to combine. Cook, stirring and tossing, for another 1 to 2 minutes. Transfer to a platter, sprinkle with salt and pepper, and add another drizzle of olive oil, if you like.

Green Bean Salad

10 MINUTES · *serves 4*

1 pound green beans, blanched and cut into 2-inch pieces

½ pound cherry tomatoes, cut in halves or quarters if larger

2 tablespoons torn mint leaves, divided

2 tablespoons chopped dill, divided

1 tablespoon olive oil

1 teaspoon red wine vinegar

2 to 3 tablespoons sheep's milk feta, crumbled

2 tablespoons toasted pistachios, chopped

Salt, to taste

Freshly ground black pepper, to taste

Toss the green beans, tomatoes, and one tablespoon each of the mint and dill in a salad bowl, then drizzle in the olive oil and vinegar and toss to combine. Top with the feta and pistachios, then sprinkle with salt and pepper and remaining mint and dill. Serve.

Quick Cucumber Salad

5 MINUTES · *serves 4*

1 to 2 cucumbers, peeled, seeded, and cut into half-moons

Splash of red wine vinegar

Flaky salt (like Maldon), to taste

1 teaspoon chopped dill

Sheep's milk feta

Toss cucumbers with vinegar, salt, dill, and a sprinkle of feta cheese.

SEASONAL SALADS

FOR ME, SALADS = IMPROVISATION. They're a chance to play with color, texture, and the different flavors in seasonal ingredients. Here are four of my seasonal faves—but don't be shy. A salad can be a great way to introduce your family to lesser-known veggies like watermelon radishes, kohlrabi, jicama, and the like. You never know when you'll stumble on a new favorite combination.

WINTER

Celery-Fennel Salad

5 MINUTES · *serves 4*

2 to 3 celery stalks, thinly sliced on the bias (leaves reserved)

1 medium fennel bulb, cored and very thinly sliced

Scant tablespoon olive oil

Juice of ¼ lemon, plus more to taste

Salt, to taste

2 to 3 tablespoons parsley leaves

2 to 3 tablespoons shaved parmesan

Freshly ground black pepper, to taste

Arrange the celery and fennel slices in an overlapping pattern on a small platter or in a small shallow bowl. Drizzle with olive oil and lemon juice. Sprinkle with salt, followed by parsley leaves, torn celery leaves, and parmesan. Finish with a little more salt and pepper.

SPRING

Bibb Salad

5 MINUTES · *serves 4*

1 medium head bibb lettuce, torn into bite-size pieces

1 medium fennel bulb, cored and very thinly sliced

3 to 4 radishes, thinly sliced

¼ cup toasted almonds, chopped

¼ cup Lemon-Chive Vinaigrette (see pg. 276)

2 ounces goat cheese, crumbled

Salt, to taste

Freshly ground black pepper, to taste

Toss the lettuce with the fennel, radishes, and almonds. Add 2 to 3 tablespoons of vinaigrette and toss again. Add more as desired (you'll have dressing left over—save it in the fridge for future salads). Crumble the goat cheese over the top, followed by a sprinkle of salt and pepper.

Simple Summer Salad

5 MINUTES · *serves 4*

- 1 small head romaine lettuce, chopped into ½-inch pieces
- ¼ cup mint leaves
- ¼ cup parsley leaves
- 1 large tomato, cored and chopped into ½-inch pieces
- 1 cucumber, peeled, seeded, and cut into ½-inch pieces
- 2 tablespoons olive oil
- 1 to 2 tablespoons lemon juice
- Flaky salt, like Maldon, to taste

Toss the romaine with the mint, parsley, tomato, and cucumber. Add the olive oil and toss to coat. Add the lemon juice and sprinkle with salt. Taste and adjust seasoning as needed.

Autumn Salad

5 MINUTES · *serves 4*

- 2 cups mixed greens
- 1 pear, cored and cut into ¼-inch slices
- ¼ cup toasted pumpkin seeds
- 2 tablespoons olive oil
- Splash of red wine or sherry vinegar
- Salt, to taste
- Freshly ground black pepper, to taste
- 2 ounces goat cheese

Combine the mixed greens, pear, and pumpkin seeds in the salad bowl and toss with the olive oil until the salad leaves are coated. Add the vinegar and toss again. Add salt and pepper to taste and toss. Top with crumbled goat cheese.

VINAIGRETTES & SAUCES

FROM VINAIGRETTES to yogurt or nut-based sauces, when you have a few solid recipes up your sleeve, it's easy to make simple food taste even more delicious. Here are a few of my favorites.

Grain Mustard Vinaigrette

10 MINUTES · *makes about 1 cup*

YOU CAN MAKE THIS all-purpose vinaigrette with all olive oil or swap in something more neutral, like canola or safflower, for half of the olive oil. Use dijon mustard in place of whole grain for a tarter, more refined dressing.

¼ cup white wine vinegar

2 tablespoons whole-grain mustard

¾ teaspoon sugar

½ teaspoon salt

Freshly ground black pepper, to taste

¾ cup olive oil

In a small jar with a lid, combine the vinegar, mustard, sugar, salt, and pepper. Cover the jar and shake until the ingredients are combined. Slowly add the oil, then cover the jar again and shake vigorously until the vinaigrette has emulsified. Taste and adjust seasoning. This vinaigrette will keep in the refrigerator for about a week.

Lemon-Chive Vinaigrette

10 MINUTES · *makes about 1 cup*

FOR A MORE MELLOW EFFECT, skip the chives and add a little more honey.

¼ cup lemon juice

2 tablespoons honey

1 teaspoon dijon mustard

1 tablespoon finely chopped fresh chives

½ teaspoon salt

Freshly ground black pepper, to taste

¼ cup olive oil

½ cup safflower or canola oil

In a small jar with a lid, combine the lemon juice, honey, mustard, chives, salt, and pepper. Cover the jar and shake until the ingredients are combined. Add the oils and shake until the vinaigrette has emulsified. Taste and adjust seasoning.

Herby Yogurt Sauce

5 MINUTES · *makes about 1 cup*

PLAIN WHOLE MILK YOGURT is a magic ingredient. Thinned, it can take the place of buttermilk for pancakes, waffles, scones, muffins, and so on. I also love to take yogurt in a savory direction—I use it for salad dressings, marinades, and vegetable dips. Here, I mix it with dill, but there are so many different herbs that work well: marjoram, oregano, chervil, and thyme are all great here. You can add a smidge of garlic pounded into a purée to give it an even deeper flavor.

1 cup plain whole milk yogurt

½ teaspoon salt, plus more to taste

2 to 3 tablespoons chopped dill

1 tablespoon lemon juice

Freshly ground black pepper, to taste

Stir all ingredients together in a small bowl, then taste and adjust seasoning. Refrigerate until ready to serve.

Tahini Sauce

5 MINUTES · *makes ½ cup*

YOU CAN NEVER HAVE TOO MUCH of this rich sauce hanging around. Drizzle it over every vegetable you can think of, thin it out with more hot water and lemon to dress a salad, layer it on the bottom of a grain bowl, or spoon it over grilled meat.

¼ cup tahini

¼ cup boiling water, plus more if needed

1 small garlic clove, peeled

Salt, to taste

2 tablespoons lemon juice, plus more to taste

Combine the tahini and boiling water in a small bowl and whisk until smooth. In a mortar and pestle or with the side of your knife on a cutting board, mash the garlic clove with a pinch of salt until it becomes a paste. Stir into the tahini along with the lemon juice. If the sauce is too thick or seems a little curdled, whisk in another splash of water. Season to taste with salt and lemon juice.

Roasted Red Pepper Salsa

10 MINUTES · *makes about 1 cup*

2 roasted red bell peppers

1 large ripe tomato, peeled and cored

½ small red onion, diced

Juice and zest of 1 lime

¼ cup chopped fresh cilantro

½ teaspoon salt, plus more to taste

Put the roasted peppers in a food processor along with the tomato, onions, and lime juice and zest and blend into a slightly chunky sauce. Transfer to a bowl and stir in the cilantro and salt to taste. Adjust seasoning if needed. This salsa will keep in the refrigerator for about 5 days.

BEANS ARE THE BEST

I'M A BEAN PUSHER. If you haven't noticed, they're among my favorite things to eat and I want everyone to love them as much as I do. Here are a few tried-and-true, child-approved (at least once) bean dishes for you to push on your nearest and dearest.

Stovetop Baked Beans

30 MINUTES · *serves 4*

2 slices of bacon, cut into 1-inch pieces

½ medium yellow onion, chopped

1 medium garlic clove, peeled and chopped

1 tablespoon tomato paste

¼ teaspoon ground cinnamon

¼ teaspoon ground cumin

½ teaspoon salt, plus more to taste

15-ounce can pinto beans, drained

2 tablespoons molasses

2 tablespoons ketchup

1 tablespoon apple cider vinegar

Freshly ground black pepper, to taste

Place the bacon in a medium saucepan over medium heat. Cook, turning occasionally, until the bacon is browned and has rendered most of its fat. Transfer bacon to a paper-towel lined plate, drain off all but 1 tablespoon of fat from the pan, and add the onions. Cook, stirring, until onions have softened, 3 to 5 minutes.

Add the garlic and cook for another minute. Add the tomato paste and cook, stirring, for 1 to 2 minutes. Add the cinnamon, cumin, and salt and cook, stirring, for another 1 to 2 minutes. Add the beans and stir to coat in the onions and spices. Add the molasses, ketchup, and vinegar and bring to a simmer, stirring occasionally, until the mixture reduces and thickens, 15 to 20 minutes. Stir in the browned bacon, season to taste, and serve warm.

My Favorite French Lentils

30 MINUTES · *serves 6*

COOK A BATCH OF LENTILS and you'll use them all week long. I often make a batch, toss them with just a splash of vinegar to store them, and dress them in the vinaigrette and other ingredients right before serving. I never tire of these!

2 cups lentils du Puy (a.k.a. French lentils)

2 cloves garlic, peeled

1 bay leaf

2 to 3 thyme sprigs (optional)

1 teaspoon salt, plus more to taste

½ cup Grain Mustard Vinaigrette (pg. 276)

1 fennel bulb, cored and diced

½ cup chopped fresh parsley leaves

½ cup chopped mint leaves

¼ cup Pickled Red Onions, chopped (pg. 270)

½ cup fresh goat cheese, crumbled

Olive oil, for drizzling

Flaky salt, for garnish

Red pepper flakes

Place the lentils in a colander and rinse with cold water, picking out any shriveled specimens or pebbles. Place in a large saucepan along with the garlic, bay leaf, and thyme, and add enough water to cover by about an inch. Bring to a simmer, uncovered, over medium-high heat, then reduce heat to medium-low. Add the salt and cook for 15 to 20 minutes, until the lentils are tender but haven't lost their shape. Drain and discard the garlic, bay, and thyme. Rinse the lentils under cold water and place in the refrigerator to cool.

When the lentils are cool, pour in the vinaigrette and stir to combine. Add the fennel, parsley, mint (reserving a little of each for garnish), and pickled onions. Adjust seasoning to taste, adding more salt or a splash of red wine vinegar if needed. Transfer to a serving bowl and sprinkle on the goat cheese and the remaining herbs. Drizzle with a little olive oil and finish with a pinch of flaky salt and red pepper flakes. Serve cold or at room temperature.

Note: this salad improves as it sits, but don't add the mint until just before you're ready to serve.

Chickpea Salad

10 MINUTES · *serves 4*

1 cup chickpeas (canned is fine)

1 medium cucumber, peeled, seeded, and cut into ½-inch pieces

½ red bell pepper, seeded and diced

4 ounces sheep's milk feta, crumbled

1 tablespoon olive oil

1 teaspoon sherry vinegar or red wine vinegar

2 tablespoons chopped parsley

2 tablespoons torn mint leaves

½ teaspoon ground sumac

¼ teaspoon smoked paprika

½ teaspoon salt, plus more to taste

Freshly ground black pepper, to taste

Place all ingredients in a medium bowl, toss to combine, then taste and adjust seasoning as needed.

Classic Hummus

10 MINUTES · *serves 4*

HOMEMADE HUMMUS has been a staple in my kitchen for as long as I've had a food processor. Even when time is tight, I add it to my list because I know how far it can take me through the week. I like to add roasted veggies to the mix—particularly when I already have some prepped and ready to go. (I can't resist a beet version with that assertive fuchsia hue.) Since hummus is pretty much always in the fridge, I often bring it out with some raw sliced veggies to curb the hangries before dinner hits the table.

1¾ cups chickpeas (cooked from dry or 15-ounce can)

½ cup tahini

1 garlic clove, chopped

4 tablespoons lemon juice

¼ cup ice water

⅛ teaspoon smoked paprika (optional)

¼ teaspoon red pepper flakes

½ teaspoon salt, or more as needed, to taste

Olive oil, for serving

Put the chickpeas in a food processor fitted with a steel blade and pulse until they're coarsely puréed. Add the tahini, garlic, and lemon juice and pulse to combine. Slowly add the water as needed to thin the hummus (you probably won't need the entire amount). Blend until smooth. Transfer to a bowl and stir in the paprika (if using), pepper flakes, and salt. Adjust seasoning to taste. Serve at room temperature drizzled with olive oil alongside pita and sliced veggies (cucumbers, carrots, fennel, red peppers, etc).

For Beet Hummus: Add ½ cup peeled chopped roasted red beets (from 2 medium beets or about 4 small beets) to the hummus after coarsely grinding the chickpeas. Proceed with the recipe as directed.

For Carrot Hummus: Add ½ cup roasted chopped carrots (about 3 to 4 medium carrots) to the hummus after coarsely grinding the chickpeas. Increase the amount of pepper flakes to ½ teaspoon.

HOW TO...

...Hard-boil an egg

SOMETIMES I MAKE a dozen hard-boiled eggs at a time; they're handy snacks to have around. As a general dinnertime rule, I make at least enough to serve each person two eggs. I like my yolks a smidge jammy and undercooked, so if you like yours firmer, add a few minutes to the total time.

Carefully place the eggs into a large saucepan. Cover with cold water, then slowly bring to a boil. As soon as the water begins to boil, turn off the heat and cover the eggs. Let sit for 8 to 12 minutes (8 for jammy yolks, 12 for firmer yolks), then drain and refill the pot with cold water. Cool the eggs in the water, drain, and refrigerate until ready to use.

...Prepare rice

Brown rice: I often add brown rice to salads or soups for my lunch and spin leftovers into fried rice, so I always make a double batch, starting with two cups of dry rice. Rinse under cold water in a fine-mesh strainer until the water runs clear. Transfer to a medium saucepan with a tight-fitting lid along with 4 cups of water and a pinch of salt. Bring to a boil, reduce heat to a low simmer, cover, and cook for about 45 minutes. When the rice is done, turn off the heat and let sit, covered, for about 10 minutes. Fluff with a fork and cover until ready to serve.

Sushi and basmati rice: Rinse 2 cups dry rice under cold water in a fine-mesh strainer until the water runs clear. Transfer to a medium saucepan with a tight-fitting lid along with 4 cups of water and a pinch of salt. Bring to a boil, reduce to a low simmer, cover, and cook for about 15 minutes or until the rice has absorbed all of the water. Turn off the heat. For sushi rice, add 2 tablespoons rice wine vinegar and cover again. Let rice sit for about 10 minutes. Fluff with a fork and transfer to a bowl.

...Drain tofu

Line a dinner plate with a double layer of paper towels and place the tofu in the center. Place a small skillet or plate on top of the tofu and weigh it down with a can of beans or a similar pantry item to press excess liquid out of the tofu. After about 15 minutes, remove the weights, discard the paper towels, and pat the tofu dry. Cut it into ½-inch cubes and transfer to a paper towel-lined colander. Pat the cubes dry one last time before cooking.

...Make crostini

Heat the oven to 375°F. Slice your favorite crusty bread into ½-inch slices, then slice in half. On a rimmed baking sheet, toss the bread with a splash of olive oil and sprinkle with salt. Place in the oven and bake until the bread is golden brown around the edges, 8 to 10 minutes.

...Grill bread

Rub thick-cut slices of bread with olive oil and grill for 1 to 2 minutes per side.

...Make guacamole

A QUICK AND EASY avocado delivery vehicle. Don't overdo it on the garlic—a little goes a long way.

1 small garlic clove, peeled

½ teaspoon salt

2 ripe avocadoes, halved and pitted

Juice of one lime

1 teaspoon chopped white onion

1 teaspoon minced cilantro

1 teaspoon minced chile pepper

In a mortar and pestle or with the side of your knife, mash the garlic and a generous pinch of salt into a smooth paste. Scoop the avocadoes into a medium-sized bowl and mash roughly with a fork. Add the garlic paste, then stir and mash to combine. Add the lime juice and stir to combine. Taste and add more salt and lime juice if needed. Garnish with chopped onion and cilantro and chile pepper.

...Make pizza dough

I COMMITTED THIS RECIPE by Mark Bittman to memory the first time I made it. It's as simple as it gets, and the super-fresh dough is really a treat.

1 teaspoon instant yeast

3 cups all-purpose flour

1½ to 2 teaspoons salt

1 cup water, plus more if needed

2 tablespoons olive oil, plus more for oiling the bowl

Whisk together the yeast, flour, and salt in the bowl of a stand mixer fitted with the dough hook. Add the water and olive oil. Mix on low for 1 minute to combine the ingredients. If the dough seems dry, add more water, a little at a time. Increase the mixer's speed to medium and knead with the dough hook for 5 to 7 minutes, until the dough is smooth and stretchy and has pulled away from the sides of the bowl.

Transfer the dough to a floured work surface and knead a few times. Shape into a ball and place in a large oiled bowl. Turn to coat and cover the bowl with plastic wrap. Let the dough rise in a draft-free spot for 1 to 2 hours, or do a slow rise in the refrigerator overnight.

LEIGH BELANGER is a food writer, editor, and recipe developer who has been enthusiastically cooking since she was a teenager. She studied gastronomy at Boston University and is the author of the *Boston Homegrown Cookbook*. Her writing and recipes have been featured in *Culture* magazine (where she was the food editor), the *Boston Globe*, *Edible Boston*, and other publications. She is the founder of Salt & Lemons, a kitchen coaching service designed to inspire and teach people to cook more at home. She lives and cooks in Boston with her husband and two boys.

Find Leigh's recipes and writing at **saltandlemons.net**.

Index